CHRISTIANITY
A DEATH AND A RESURRECTION

DEBRA WROBLEWSKI

xulon
PRESS

Copyright © 2014 by Debra Wroblewski

Christianity
A Death and A Resurrection
by Debra Wroblewski

Printed in the United States of America

ISBN 9781629527345

All rights reserved solely by the author. The author guarantees all contents are original and do not infringe upon the legal rights of any other person or work. No part of this book may be reproduced in any form without the permission of the author. The views expressed in this book are not necessarily those of the publisher.

Unless otherwise indicated, Bible quotations are taken from the King James Version of the Bible, *Public Domain*.

www.xulonpress.com

TABLE OF CONTENTS

1. The Purpose of Christianity 19
2. The Holy Bible and the origin of Christianity 22
3. God, Who is He? Who is Jesus Christ? Who is the Holy Spirit? What about the Trinity 26
4. Creation of Man 38
5. Satan 43
6. The Garden of Eden and The Fall 47
7. Sin 51
8. Salvation, Redemption 57
9. Salvation is Through None Other than Jesus Christ 71
10. Born Again—Our Birthright 79
11. What is Faith? 97
12. Walking After the Spirit Not After the Flesh 99
13. Eternal Security 104
14. Who We Are In Christ 121
15. The Power and/or Authority in Us 130
16. The Enemy and Warfare 134
17. Prayer 138
18. The Lord's Supper or The Eucharist 143
Questions to ponder by chapter 147
Appendix 1 – Reference Page 157
Appendix 2 – Other Names of God 159
Appendix 3 – The True Character of Christians 161
Appendix 4 – The Benefits of the New Nature 163

PREFACE

What is the purpose of Christianity? Does it have any significance? Where and when did the concept of Christianity begin? What's it about? How does one become a Christian; are there requirements? Why is it that so many people who say they are Christians look and act just like those don't know Christ and don't seem to care if they are, or aren't? Why the many different denominations? How can you tell who is a Christian? Who are God, Jesus and The Holy Spirit? What is Baptism and what does it have to do with Christianity? What about Communion or the Eucharist? What is sin? Who is the Devil? What does he do? Is there any victory in this life? These have been over riding questions for me. WHAT IS THE TRUTH? These are things we will explore through Scripture in this book.

Who am I that I should write a book about truth? I have no special education, no degrees, no following. It was early one morning in my quiet time that I was impressed to write this book, and when I asked the Holy Spirit that question, this is what came into my mind: It was said of Peter and John in Acts 4:13 after they had healed the paralytic man when the religious leaders of their day; *"perceived that they were uneducated and untrained men, they marveled, and they realized that they had been with Jesus."* So to answer, I have questioned truth to the point of research, my hunger for the truth has led me to the place I was willing to forsake the little church doctrine I was taught, popular rhetoric and religious 'counsel' to find it. In my search I went to the Holy Spirit who the Bible said is our teacher. I have spent much time with the Holy Spirit, questioning, studying and listening to find the answers. I do not claim to know all the truth for the Word of God says, *"we see through a glass darkly, but then we shall know even as we are known."* Nor will I say this will be the final revelation I receive from the Holy Spirit since there have been many revisions. As I write I have gained greater understanding. Neither will I say that I have total victory in every area of my life, I am still in battle and still learning to apply what I have learned as I continue my search for truth. However, due to the crucial message and closing of time as we know it I feel it is important to close this work and let each of you who take the time to read and study this message to let the Holy Spirit teach you through the Word. God is not a respecter of persons and He will grant each one who earnestly seeks Him revelation.

INTRODUCTION

Christianity is a PROCESS and as with any process there are continually new revelations. I feel I am only beginning my journey of truth. It is with much trepidation that I write this book. God is a Holy God and will not be mocked. How can you condense the Word of God when He has said *'not one jot or tittle will pass away until all is fulfilled?'* That means not one dotting of an 'I' or one crossing of a 'T' of the Word of God will be made null and void until everything has been fulfilled. This work is an attempt to give you as much truth as possible with as few words as possible. With this in mind I have used a lot of the Holy Scriptures, King James Version except stated otherwise, and many definitions from both Webster's Dictionary and the Strong's Exhaustive Concordance and few of my own words. It is with sincere awe and great reverence that I have poured over this material time and time again so as not to misquote nor alter any word from within the context which I have taken the Scripture. I do not offer this work lightly, because the souls of humanity are at stake.

It *IS* possible for every person to know the truth and live it, *IF* they would spend the time and effort studying and asking the Holy Spirit to give them understanding and wisdom as they study the Holy Scripture and apply the Word to their lives. Paul in Colossians 2:2-3, while bringing encouragement to the Colossians states: *"that their hearts may be encouraged, being knit together in love, and **attaining to all** riches of the **full assurance of understanding, to the knowledge of the mystery of God**, both of the Father and of Christ, **in whom are hidden all the treasures of wisdom and knowledge."***

Again I will reiterate that I do not claim to know all there is about God and His Word, nor the fullness of what Salvation entails. As a believer *'all the treasures of wisdom and knowledge are mine in Christ Jesus'* according to the previously stated Scripture. I believe we as Christians have so misunderstood the awesome God we serve and the awesome knowledge and power available to us. I have grown weary of seeing the Word of God misused as reference to build up certain doctrinal viewpoints which has brought much error in the Christian community. The 'world' blasphemes the name of our Lord and Savior, Jesus Christ, because of 'Christian's' failure to deliberately and adequately *'WALK'* in His truth. In Hosea 4:6 the Word says, *'My people are destroyed for lack of knowledge. <u>Because you have rejected knowledge</u>, I will also reject you from being priest for Me; <u>Because you have forgotten the law of your God, I also will forget your children</u>.'* Here God is speaking to His prophets and or priests; Christians are called a holy priesthood in 1 Peter 2:5 so as Christians when we reject the full council of Scripture we are rejecting God's Word and therefore set ourselves up to be rejected by Him.

I have written in the following format in an attempt to give understanding to those who are desperately seeking the truth and possibly bring light to some error in the body of Christ. We, as Christians have not *'brought up our children in the way they SHOULD go'* nor have we taught those within our spiritual influence the truth straight from the Word of God, resulting in many who profess Christianity, yet fail to produce the 'fruit' of it. We have laid aside the Bible and used Doctrinal biased curriculum to teach in our Bible study classes and 'Sunday School' classes, Biblical Seminaries and Universities. And unbeknown to us have either never come to know the truth or have lost our way. It's as if we are not yet out of the 'Dark Ages' of truth. Again, in saying this I am not professing to be the only true follower of Jesus Christ nor do I think that I am above any other person on the road to truth; my desire is to only state the truth from the Word of God without doctrinal bias.

To those who pick this study up and feel it is too elementary for your levels of Scriptural understanding please do not lay it aside; there may be yet something within the context of this book which may open your eyes to a truth you have not yet seen. It is no accident that you have obtained it. God may yet have you learn something from my simplistic approach. I have written in this format so that those who may read it who have no knowledge of God, His Word or His plan of Salvation may come to the knowledge of the truth and be saved and for those who have been in 'the church' for years and yet walk as the 'world' walks may come to knowledge of the truth.

Bear with me through the Scriptural quotations and definitions, the repetition of Scripture and definitions are there to bring out specific points and draw the reader back to the source of truth, the Bible itself. The reason

Introduction

for putting the definitions in within the context of the Scripture; it is very important to give a complete picture of the underlying truth that is being expounded upon. It is my desire to give you a background of the most beautiful history that has been replayed throughout the ages over, and over again; sometimes so perverted by Satan himself, his minions and followers, that it is distorted beyond recognition.

All references to God, Jesus Christ and the Holy Spirit are capitalized.

This is a study, not just a book to be casually read. As you get into it you will begin to see just how important it is to understand not only the history but the meaning of the words. I pray that as you study this material the Holy Spirit will draw you into the Word for your own journey of THE TRUTH. With that in mind I offer my sincere prayer that God receive all the glory because it is His work and His Word.

I had thought when I finished chapter sixteen I was finished, but the Holy Spirit took me even further. Chapter seventeen was a revelation that brought me to brokenness, for I have failed to walk in the power that is so clearly shown in Scripture. I have grown with each chapter but I believe this chapter is the crux of the whole book. I pray we begin to tarry before the LORD until we are clothed with power from on high.

DEDICATION

To The MOST HIGH GOD, *YHWH*, The Sovereign LORD, i.e. Master of the universe, The Holy One of Israel, my Elohim, my Father and my Savior; *Yashua Mashicach* (Jesus Christ), and *The Ruach Ha'Kodesh* (Holy Spirit) without whom, you nor I simply put, would not be.

I owe it all to YOU!

In Memory

In memory of my late father and mother, J.C. and Porthania Langley, who through God's grace were faithful in keeping our family in church and walking the narrow way.

My hunger for Christ came from that humble upbringing.

ACKNOWLEDGEMENTS

I would like to thank my husband, Farron, who has patiently endured my 'sharing' as I have gleaned from the Word over the years.

I want to thank my special friend Lou Jamison who read the first manuscript and gave me the encouragement to believe I could actually write. The following friends who read the 'almost' final manuscript: Kim Dunham thank you for editing and advising the latest attempt to get the manuscript ready for the publisher; your excitement got me excited. Sister Kay McGee, your thoughts expressed so exuberantly gave me the faith to believe it was truly needed. To a special friend, you blessed me so much with your review that I can't express how deeply I was moved. Thank you so much Laura Strong for giving me one last review. Thank you all for taking your precious time; I am truly humbled by your comments and reviews.

All of those at Xulon Press for their advise, patience and technical help through this process.

Chapter One

The Purpose of Christianity

Why become a Christian? Simply put because it restores life to the dead; God had told Adam and Eve if they partook of the fruit of the "Tree of the Knowledge of Good and Evil", they would surely die. Because of their disobedience (sin), every person who is born into this world is born spiritually dead. [1] At birth the process of physical death begins. Although we are physically alive, we are spiritually dead. All humanity was alienated from God by sin, the transgression of a command resulting in enmity with God. Jesus died on the cross to restore life to man. [2] His desire is that man's relationship be restored and that man may again be holy and blameless, beyond reproach in His sight. [3] Because of God's mercy and love, He did what could not be done by human effort to restore the relationship severed by Adam and Eve. It is God's desire that man be adopted into His family, [4] and that He may have many sons in glory: [5] therefore Christians are to imitate God as His children. [6] It is God's desire that Christians GROW UP into Him. [7] Through Jesus Christ, God the Father has provided everything a person needs for life and godliness, and it is His desire to bestow His divine nature on all who come to Him. [8]

Why is it so important? The entire world recognizes there are two forces in the universe; the force of evil and the force of good. Every nation, every culture and every religion recognizes these two forces. The theme behind every story (novel, fairy tale, myth, etc.), every movie and every action of man depicts one or both of these opposing forces. The Bible tells us who these forces are; Jesus Christ, the force of good and Satan, the force of evil.

Jesus Christ has made it possible for all things to be subdued through His death and resurrection by destroying the devil [9] and disarming principalities and powers. [10] He (Jesus) is now sitting at the right hand of the Father. [11] He waits until all things are made subject to Him. [12] He made Christians His ambassadors on the earth. [13] As Christians submit their lives to Him, the kingdom of God will come in the earth as it is in heaven. [14]

The Christian, as the body of Christ, is to reveal the exceeding, great, and diverse wisdom of God to the mutant, fallen spirits of disobedience, which now have controlling influence or power over all the earth, causing chaos and destruction. [15] As ambassadors for Christ, we are to be trained in government [16] and spiritual warfare [17] to co-rule with Christ as Bride: [18] that all things may be restored back to the Father. [19]

What significance does it have today? All creation is awaiting the redemption of man because the creation itself will also be redeemed. [20] Neither heaven nor earth will pass away until every dot and stroke of the Word of God is fulfilled, [21] and when all things are one in Christ, both in heaven and in earth. [22]

Everyone must appear before the judgment seat of Christ so that each one will be recompensed for their deeds done in the body, whether good or bad. [23] Therefore as we are made ambassadors of Christ we are to compel others to be reconciled to God. [24] *"For the wrath of God is being revealed from heaven against all ungodliness and unrighteousness of men who suppress the truth in un-righteousness."* [25] The gospel of Christ is the power of God, for salvation to everyone who will believe. [26] Christians are to be filled with the Holy Spirit so that the power of God will be manifested in them that they may bring many sons to glory [27] and, most importantly, to restore the relationship between God and man. Adam and Eve had walked and talked with God in the Garden of Eden in the cool of the day. That relationship with God was severed when they partook of the fruit of the 'tree of the knowledge of good and evil". [28] Through Jesus Christ, man's relationship with God can be restored and thus once again walk and talk with God.

CHAPTER ONE

[1] 1 Corinthians 15:22
[2] Ephesians 2: 1, 4, 5
[3] Colossians 1:21-23
[4] Galatians 4:5 & Ephesians 1:5
[5] Hebrews 2:10
[6] Ephesians 5:1
[7] Ephesians 4:15
[8] 2 Peter 1:3 & 4
[9] Hebrews 2:14
[10] Colossians 2:15
[11] Colossians 3:1, Mark 14:62
[12] 1 Corinthians 15:25-28
[13] 2 Corinthians 5:20
[14] Matthew 6:10
[15] Ephesians 3:10
[16] Matthew 25:21, Luke 22:28-30, 1 Corinthians 6:2-3
[17] Ephesians 6:12, 2 Corinthians 10:4 & 6:7, 1 Timothy 1:18, 2 Timothy 2:1-4, 10
[18] 2 Corinthians 11:2, Ephesians 6:22-23, Revelation 21:9 & 22:17
[19] 1 Corinthians 15:28, Colossians 1:13-20
[20] Romans 8:19-21, 23
[21] Matthew 5:18
[22] Ephesians 1:10
[23] 2 Corinthians 5:9-10
[24] 2 Corinthians 5:18-20
[25] Romans 1:18[8]
[26] Romans 1:16
[27] Romans 8:3-4 & 2 Thessalonians 1:11-12
[28] Genesis 3:8

Chapter Two

The Holy Bible and The Origin of Christianity

The Bible is the *INSPIRED*, literally 'God breathed,' history of man and revelation of Himself to His creation. The Creator, Elohim, inspired certain men to write of His Life, His character, His precepts, His plan and His laws so that we may know Him. It is the history and the only book to record the origin of the heavens, earth, man and his existence. It IS history, it is His-story, literally God's own story of His involvement with man. It is history from God's perspective to the people He chose to bring the revelation of Himself to the world, namely the nation of Israel.

Just how did we get the Bible? As previously stated; by the inspiration of God through the Holy Spirit during the course of almost 1900 years from over forty men of various back-grounds, some with no 'formal' education. Among them were prophets, poets, tentmakers, shepherds, kings, governors, carpenters, fishermen, tax collectors, doctors, scribes and musicians, and as one friend reminded me 'a burning bush.' It was given by oral communication-God Himself speaking to man, inspiration-through thoughts and meditation upon God Himself and revelation-revealing Himself through provision, protection, creation itself, as well as through dreams and visions.

How can we know that it is true? What is there that confirms that it is indeed *the real thing*? As Chaplain DeWhitt of the Arkansas Dept. of Prisons, McPherson Unit, says, "Truth is visible, it can be seen." So, prophecy and fulfillment (visible proof) of the prophecies contained within the Bible itself. There are over three hundred prophecies in the

Old Testament concerning Jesus alone. Some were hundreds and thousands of years before His birth, yet they were all fulfilled and documented in the New Testament. These prophecies began with the first book of the Bible and continued to the last book of the Old Testament. The book of Revelation is just that-*The Revelation of Jesus Christ*-what was and is and is to come. The future return of Jesus Christ has been prophesied and will come to pass at just the right time. There are prophecies concerning the rise and fall of nations. There are many prophecies concerning the nation of Israel that have been and are being fulfilled even to this present day. Of all the prophecies of the Bible only those in regard to the end time events; the tribulation, Coming of Christ in His glory to set up His Kingdom with ten thousands of His saints and the final judgment of the devil and his hordes of demons with all who have followed them to destruction have yet to be fulfilled. Some are being fulfilled on a daily basis, drawing us closer to His return.

If you do not believe the Bible is not only the inspired Word of God, but completely true, you cannot be a Christian. Without belief in The Sovereign GOD of the Bible, Jesus Christ and the Holy Spirit one cannot be a Christian. I can say this because *"God is not a man that He should lie,"* [1] EITHER ALL OF IT IS TRUE OR NONE OF IT IS TRUE. The Holy Bible must be taken as a whole, you cannot take part if it as true and exclude some as just a myth or fable. It is God's Son, Jesus Christ incarnate (God come in the flesh) that is the basis of Christianity. The word Christian means Christ like.

The Bible is cohesive; it is built line upon line, precept upon precept [2] There is no other book or manual; no other place you can go to get all the instruction you need in finding out how to become and maintain your Christianity and your life. Other books, such as this one, will help you to better understand Christianity. You cannot use them exclusively, nor should you use them at all if they do not agree completely-100% with the Holy Bible or if they are not referenced from the Bible. If anything they teach is not in complete accord with the WHOLE COUNSEL of The Holy Bible they are of no use. The Bible does not contradict itself. There are those who take Scripture out of context and use it as if it did. By context I mean within the Chapter and Book of the Bible the Scripture is contained. You cannot take one Scripture or several Scriptures and base a doctrine or belief system upon them if they do not agree with the whole counsel of Scripture. If there appears to be a contradiction, it is because it is not fully understood within the context which it is written or has not been studied from both Old and New Testament concerning that matter. Should you take a certain verse and begin to build a belief system without considering what the whole Bible has to say on that subject, it would be like taking a manual for heart surgery and using only part of it and trying to perform a heart surgery. It must be used as a whole. The Bible has been preserved as is for the last two thousand years for the purpose of giving a clear understanding of what it means to follow Jesus Christ.

Someone recently asked me, "What was the purpose of the removal of the Apocryphal Books?" According to Finis Jennings Dakes in *God's Plan for Man*, and many other sources the litmus test contained fourteen statements such as: "They did not pass the test required of inspired books, they were not accepted by a prophet, the Jews did not recognize them as inspired, they were never quoted nor recognized by Christ or the Apostles, Divine authority was never claimed by the authors, they were self-contradictory and opposed to doctrines of Scripture, Josephus did not regard them as Scripture, they were only added after 300 A.D. and rejected at the Laodicean Council in 363 A.D. and the last one I will mention here is The last Old Testament prophet predicted the next messenger to come to Israel from God would be the forerunner of Christ,[3] the Apocryphal books were written during the period between Malachi and Christ." John the Baptist was the forerunner of Christ that had come in the Spirit of Elijah.[4]

The Bible is the 'Owner's Manual' of humanity. What manufacturer would build something and not supply an instruction manual of not only how to use it but what it is made of, a parts list if you will? I've often heard it said of a baby, "If they only came with instructions!" Well, they have, but we have laid it aside and used 'common sense' or the 'wisdom of the world' to raise them. The Bible is the guide with which we can not only know what we are made of but how best to live as well.

Based on The Holy Bible, God Himself is the originator of Christianity; it began in the heart and mind of God before the creation of the world. *"For he chose **us** in Him (Christ Jesus) before the creation of the world to be holy and blameless in His sight."* [5] Notice '*chose us in Him BEFORE the CREATION of the WORLD*'. Jesus Christ is the Lamb referred to in Revelation 13:8; "*the Lamb that was slain from the creation of the world.*" Again, note who was '*slain **from the creation of the world**.*' Hence, Christianity began in the heart and mind of God before the earth was created. Of the word *Lamb*: John says*: "The next day John saw Jesus coming toward him, and said, "Behold! The Lamb of God who takes away the sin of the world."* [6] And again, *"knowing that you were not redeemed with corruptible things, like silver or gold, from your aimless conduct* *received by tradition from your fathers,* **but with the precious blood of Christ, as of a lamb** *without blemish and without spot."* [7]

So where did the thought of Christianity come from? The Creator explains *"**He** (God, the Father) **predestined us to be adopted as His sons through Jesus Christ, <u>in accordance with His pleasure and will</u>"*—.[8] So Elohim (GOD), the Creator instituted Christianity, before the foundation of the world according to His pleasure and will. Christianity is God's plan to bring man back into relationship with Himself, the Creator, through the death of His Son.

CHAPTER TWO

[1] Numbers 23:19
[2] Isaiah 28:10
[3] Malachi 3:1[11]
[4] Matthew 11:13-14
[5] Ephesians 1:4
[6] John 1:29
[7] 1 Peter 1:18-19[8]
[8] Ephesians 1:5[4]

Chapter Three

God, Who is He? Who is Jesus Christ? Who is the Holy Spirit? What about the Trinity?

Who is God?

Before I begin to answer these questions, let me start by saying as the Apostle John said in John 21:25; *"And there are also many other things which Jesus did, the which if they should be written every one, I suppose that even the world itself could not contain the books which were written."* The universe could not possibly contain the complete knowledge of God so this is just a minute, very concise description of His Majesty. God is Sovereign over all things; there is only one thing out of His control. [1] He has chosen to give man authority over his own life. God is Love personified; His love is so great that He's not willing for even the vilest sinner to perish, but He is totally 'Just' in that if they refuse to repent and turn to Him, He must exact the punishment due them (wage of their sin). He is Holy which means sacred. Righteous, i.e. a God of equity meaning it is His inherent nature to be righteousness; He can do nothing against that inherent nature of righteousness.

The heart of God is LOVE, a Father's love. It is God's revealed desire to be 'Our' Father above all else. When we read through the Old Testament we see Him moving in the lives of certain people; those who were attentive enough to hear God when He revealed Himself to them. The second record of God interacting with man after Adam and Eve were cast from the Garden of Eden, was Enoch, in Genesis 5:22 -24. Enoch and God had such a relationship that apparently God didn't want to wait for him to die He simply took him. Enoch was the fifth generation from Adam, which spanned approximately five hundred years. Four hundred years later, Noah found grace in the eyes of God. God's love for His creation is so great He has gone to extreme measures to salvage man.

The Bible is the Revelation of God

The Bible being His revelation to man of Himself; I would like to list a few of the names in which God revealed Himself to us and their Biblical references. We will discuss the attributes of some of the names in this chapter. I have included the Hebrew translation where given in Scripture. From the Old Testament, Hebrew, He is the Creator *'Elohim'* meaning Almighty Deity. [2] *The Holy One*, [3] *The Sovereign-YAHWEH*. [4] *I Am-YAH, He told Moses*. [5] *'The Alpha and Omega' (Greek trans-lation) meaning, The Beginning and The End, i.e., The 'Aleph and Tav'*, *which is the Hebrew translation*. [6] He is *'The Infinite'-El Elyon, meaning God Most High*. [7] *The Ancient of Days*, [8] *The Righteous Judge*, [9] *King of Salem*, [10] He is the Mighty God of Israel-*El Elohe Israel*, [11] *The Most High God* — Israel's *Redeemer* [12] without naming Himself, He is Omnipotent. [13] He established equity, He executes judgment and righteousness. [14]

How Biblical names were chosen

Biblical names were chosen revealing some aspect of the nature of the individual or circumstances surrounding the birth of the child, therefore, the many different names of God in the Old Testament revealed a trait or characteristic or possibly a circumstance surrounding the instance of His recognition. For example, in Genesis 29:30 when Leah gave birth to Judah, she *'praised'* the Lord; therefore she named him 'Judah' which in Hebrew means praise. When Rebekah bore Esau and Jacob, she named each one by what she saw, *"And the first came out red, all over like an hairy garment; and they called his name Esau. And after that came his brother out, and his hand took hold on Esau's heel; and his name was called Jacob."* [15] Esau literally means hairy and Jacob means supplanter or deceitful, literally *One Who Takes the Heel*. [16] So when someone had an encounter with God or when God revealed Himself or maybe came to their aid in a circumstance or situation they referred to Him by that name.

There are other times when God Himself told them 'My name is___,' as shown in Exodus 6:3 God said that He had appeared to Abraham, Isaac and Jacob as the Almighty God but they did not know Him by His name,

Jehovah (LITERALLY-<u>YHWH</u>- *Yud-Heh-Vav-Heh*, in English referred to as Y<small>AHWEH</small>). [17] But let's go back to the first time the word God is used in the Bible. The word 'God' is not His name, but a title just as 'the L<small>ORD</small>' is a title. The very opening of the Bible says, *'In the beginning G*OD *created the heavens and the earth.* [18] 'G<small>OD</small>' here is the original Hebrew word 'Elohim,' *El* meaning 'Almighty' and *HIM* is the plural word for 'deity'. The *'Elohim'* created the heavens and earth. Notice '*him*,' is plural-are there more than one God? No! But as Scripture bears-out there is actually one God expressed in multiple persons or 'essences.' *And God (singular) said, "Let Us (plural) make man in Our image, after Our likeness."* [19] Who is the 'Our' and 'Us'? *Elohim* is comprised of, God-The Father, God-The Son (Jesus Christ), and God-The Holy Spirit as it has been revealed in Scripture. How do I know that? A New Testament passage that reveals the plural unity of the *Elohim* is recorded in John where Jesus while praying for the disciples speaking to God the Father says: *"that they all may **be one; as Thou, Father, art in Me and I in Thee, that they also may be one in Us** ."* [20] Then again; .."***the Word was with God, and the Word was*** *God. The same was in the beginning **with** God."* [21] Look at Jesus' baptism by John. *"**And Jesus when He was baptized**, ...**he (John) saw the Spirit of God <u>descending</u>** like a dove and lighting upon Him, **and lo, a voice <u>from</u> heaven saying, "This is My beloved Son**, in whom I am well pleased."* [22] Jesus being baptized, the Holy Spirit is descending upon Him and God the Father is speaking from heaven.

God revealed Himself

God revealed Himself to Abram as *El Elyon*, [23] Abram's (Abraham's) nephew Lot was taken captive and Abram was told it. Abram took his personal trained servants and went against the invading army. He retrieved Lot, the people of Sodom and Gomorrah, and all their goods. When they returned, Melchizedek, King of Salem, which was priest of **God Most High**, blessed Abram. Here we are given the name of God-*El Elyon* from the original Hebrew. The Name 'God Most High' or *El Elyon* pertains to the Almighty – which is the 'highest, supreme, lofty, elevated, and exalted. *Elyon* is derived from the verb '*alah*' meaning "to ascend." [24] This is also the name used of God in Luke where the angels are praising God saying, *"Glory to **God** in the highest, peace on earth, good will toward men."* [25] The Scripture could and probably should have been translated *Glory to God Most High*. When Abram is before Melchizedek and gives Him a tithe of all he had retrieved, Abram says, *"I have raised my hand to the* L<small>ORD</small> (literally ***YHWY***), ***God Most High***, ***Possessor of heaven and earth."***

[26] I have read or heard somewhere that 'LORD' is in reference to His pre-eminence, 'God Most High' in reference to His name and 'Possessor of heaven and earth' His position. We see the name '*God Most High*' or *El Elyon* is also the name used in the book of Daniel. [27] When Moses asked, "*Who should I tell the children of Israel that has sent me?*" God said '*I AM*' – [28] In Hebrew it literally means 'I Am that I Am' or 'I Am To Be' or 'I Exist.'

The word '**LORD**' is actually a title which replaced the name of God, '**YHWY**', the Hebrew spelling of His name. The Hebrew language has only consonants in its alphabet, vowels are used only as pointers to help non Hebrew people to pronounce the words. [29] Traditionally YHWH is translated **Jehovah**, there were no 'J's in the alphabet until the early 1600's [30] so it originally would have been spelled **Yehovah** which means *Self Existent One*. So anytime you see 'the LORD' written in this way it replaces YHWY.

God Almighty is translated from **El Shaddai:** *The All Powerful, The One Who is Self-Sufficient.* [31] In Genesis 22:14, when God intervened in Abrahams sacrifice of Isaac it says Abraham called the name of the place, *YHWH Will Provide* which is translated from **Jehovah Jireh** – properly *Yeh-ho-vaw yir-eh': or God will see to it.* Another name for God in Scripture is-God **Omnipotent** or all powerful, "*Alleluia: for YHWH, (God) omnipotent reigneth.*" [32] There are two descriptions without actually using a name; He is everywhere or ***Omnipresent*** – meaning there is no where we can go to get away from Him. He is present everywhere. It cannot be too dark for us to hide, for darkness is just as if it were the light of day to God. We cannot hide in the depth of the sea or the bowels of the earth. [33] He is all knowing or ***Omniscient***; He knows it all, nothing is beyond His knowledge or finding out. [34] He knows what is in the depths of our hearts. [35] He knows every move we make, He knows our every thought. He knows all about us, when we get up or lay down, there is nothing He doesn't know or understand. He knows every word before we speak it. [36] Because He is Holy, we must not only recognize Him as holy, we should never enter His presence without respect or reverence. [37] Every priest had to sanctify himself before drawing near God so as not to incur the wrath of God. [38] Then again speaking of the priest He tells them not only were they holy but the offerings and sacrifices were to be holy. [39] He has bared His holy arm that all the earth shall see His Salvation. Jesus is the Holy Arm of God or His Salvation. [40] Not only is Gods' person, but His name as well, are set apart to be worshipped. In the first commandment He stated He is to be put first and the second they were never to speak His name idly or foolishly. [41] He alone is entitled to holy reverence. He is loyal, just and faithful. His truths are binding and He never fails. Another description is, *"The LORD (YHWH) is a man of war: the LORD (YHWH) is His name.*[42]

Other revealing attributes of God

Some other attributes of God in His Word are that He is a **God of Mercy**, showing kindness and pity, being compassionate, with a tender love or showing favor or beauty.[43] He is a God of Grace which may also mean favor and kindness but it expresses the divine influence of grace, having the implication of gratitude, joy, and the pleasure of the ones to whom it is bestowed.[44] A couple of examples are; He told Moses, I will be *gracious* and He said to Jonah, 'should I not be *gracious* to people who don't know one side from another'. In the New Testament, Peter says, 'He is found to be *gracious*.' His *grace* is revealed again in the New Testament.[45] There are over 125 names as reference for God in the Holy Bible describing some aspect of GOD, so you see these are only a few. For a picture of God which He describes Himself from all creations point of view read in Job 38 and 39 in the Holy Bible.

WHO IS JESUS?

Jesus the second 'essence' of the Godhead and the ONLY '*begotten*'[46] Son of God; the only person sired by God through the agency of the Holy Spirit. He (Jesus) was in existence before anything was created, and by His very own power keeps everything together.[47] Only through the virgin birth could Jesus be completely sinless as a man. The sin nature of man is passed down through the father.[48] God in Jesus Christ became flesh, took upon Himself flesh and blood that He might redeem mankind back to Himself.

Just as I stated earlier the letter 'J' was not in the English alphabet until the early 1600's so the spelling of His name from the Greek manuscripts would have been *'Iesus, or Ieosus'*-the proper spelling of His name in the Hebrew would be *'Yahshua'* which means; 'Yah' is salvation, Yah is the name of God shortened in several passages in the Old Testament. The name 'Jesus' has no meaning in the Greek or English.[49]

Jesus is Love in the flesh personified. In Hebrews 1:1-12, He is God's heir and He made the worlds.[50] He is the Creator. He is *'the express image of* God' and sovereignly rules all things; He supports or contains everything by His powerful Word.[51]

Yahshua i.e., Jesus is God

He cleansed us, purged sin from us. [52] He is the ultimate **High Priest**,*' who is holy, harmless, undefiled, separate from sinners, and made higher than the heavens;* He doesn't need to make sacrifices for Himself then for the people because He was sinless. He died once for all sin, [53] and sat down in His majesty in the heavens. [54] God the Father talking to Jesus His Son says: *"Thy throne, O God, is forever and ever; a scepter of righteousness is the scepter of Thy kingdom.* [55] So we see that JESUS IS **God** and king; only a king has a scepter. His scepter is a scepter of righteousness or as the Jewish Study Bible says it a scepter of equity. [56] *Thou hast loved righteousness and hated iniquity; therefore God, even Thy God, hath anointed Thee with the oil of gladness above Thy fellows."* [57] Not because He does righteous things but it is of His nature to be righteous.

Jesus revealing His Godhood and Titles

GOD INCARNATE–GOD WHO BECAME FLESH. *"And the Word became flesh, and dwelt among us, and we saw His glory, glory as of* **the only begotten from the Father***, full of grace and truth."* [58] *"****For in Him dwells all the fullness of the Godhead bodily.***" [59] *"I came forth from the Father and am come into the world: I leave the world and go to the Father."* [60] *"All things that the Father hath are mine."* [61] Jesus is 'The *I AM'*, which is **Self-Existent, Eternal One**. Jesus said, *before Abraham was, I AM."* [62] *"I Am the Bread of life,"* [63] *"I Am the Light of the world,"* [64] *"I Am from above,"* [65] *"I Am the Door,"* [66] *"I Am the Good Shepherd,"* [67] *"I Am the Resurrection and the Life,"* [68] *"I Am **The Way, The Truth** and **The Life**."* [69] Jesus is saying I am God, one and the same as the God of Moses, the God of Abraham, the God of Isaac and the God of Jacob. For this reason the Pharisees (religious leaders of the Jewish sect) were angry with Him and declared Him a blasphemer; because He was claiming to be 'The *I AM'* or God. Isaiah says, *'For to us a child is born, to us a son is given, and the government will be on his shoulders. And He will be called* **Wonderful, Counselor, Mighty God, Everlasting Father**, *and* **Prince of Peace**.' [70] The opening chapters of the Gospel of John says, *'In the beginning was the Word, and the Word was with God, and* **the Word was** *God. He was with God in the beginning.'* [71] Nothing was created without Him and He is the **Light** of men. [72] He is the **Water of Life**–*"If anyone is thirsty,* **let him come to Me and drink**. [73] He is **Our Salvation**– *Grace to you and peace from God our Father and the Lord Jesus Christ,* **who gave Himself for our sins so that He might rescue us from this present evil age***, according to the will of our God and Father,* [74] He will be extolled, worshipped in eternity for He is worthy, He was slain, and with His blood He bought us *'from every tribe and language and people and nation.'*[75] As **The Great High Priest** –He became flesh and went through everything we go through in every way so that He could be merciful and understanding, *that He might make atonement for the sins of the people.*[76] *"Therefore, holy brothers, who share in the heavenly calling, fix your thoughts on Jesus,* **the Apostle and High Priest** *whom we confess."* [77] He is the **Redeemer** by means of His ultimate sacrifice.[78] He is the **Lord of lords** and **King of kings**.[79] **The Bright and Morning Star.** [80] **Immanuel-** which means **God with us.** [81] **The Rock,**[82] **Deliverer,**[83] **Friend,**[84] **Judge,**[85] **Christ Jesus our hope** and The **Hope of Glory.** [86] All judgment is given to Jesus Christ by the Father; *"For as the Father has life in Himself, so He has granted the Son to have life in Himself, and* **has given Him authority to execute judgment** *also, because He is the Son of Man."* [87] Jesus submitted Himself to the Father by saying and doing only what the Father instructed Him to do.[88]

What He Did:

The Old Testament Tabernacle was a copy of the true tabernacle in heaven, and Jesus Christ is the revealing of the true Tabernacle, He functioned not only as the Priest but also the Sacrificial Lamb. Every piece of furniture in the Tabernacle represented a particular function that Jesus fulfilled in His life and ministry, and in doing so He destroyed the devil and his power [89] His sole purpose in coming to earth was to redeem man and purchase us back from the enemy and deliver us from the power of sin by taking it away.[90] He came as God's own Son to reign as Sovereign Lord. [91]*"Now I saw heaven opened, and behold a white horse. And He who sat on him was called Faithful and True, and* **in righteousness He judges and makes war**. *He was clothed with a robe dipped in blood, and His name is called* **The Word of God**. *And He has on His robe and on His thigh a name written:* **KING OF KINGS** *and* **LORD OF LORDS**.*"* [92]

Who is the Holy Spirit?

The Holy Spirit is the third 'essence' of the Godhead. "*Go therefore and make disciples of all nations, baptizing them in the name of the Father and the Son and **the Holy Spirit**, and teaching them to observe all that I have commanded you; and lo **I am with you always**, even to the end of the age.*" [93] Here we see that Jesus stated He would be with them always in the form of the Holy Spirit. I would like to state that 'the name' or the family name for God is YHWY or as we say it in English, Yahweh. *"For*

*God so loved the world that He gave **His only begotten Son**, that whoever believes in Him shall not perish, but have eternal life."* [94] Jesus is the only begotten of the Father. As the Holy Spirit overshadowed Mary, she conceived, just as He hovered or brooded over the face of the deep at the creation.[95] Jesus said of His crucifixion – *"Nevertheless I tell you the truth; It is expedient for you that I go away: for if I do not go away, the **Comforter** will not come unto you; but if I depart, I will send Him unto you."* [96] The Holy Spirit is The Spirit of Truth, Our Guide - *"Howbeit when He, the **Spirit of Truth**, is come, He will guide you into all truth: for He shall not speak of Himself; but whatsoever He shall hear, that He shall speak: and He will shew you things to come." He shall glorify Me: for He shall receive of Mine, and shall shew it unto you."* [97]

The Holy Spirit is our Helper and **Teacher**

Everything belongs to the Father; Jesus said the Holy Spirit would show us all things that belongs the Father. [98] The *Helper, the Holy Spirit*, will teach everything that Jesus taught, and remind us of everything Jesus said. [99] Jesus said if we loved Him we would keep His commandments and He would ask the Father to do whatever we ask, and He would ask the Father to send *'the Spirit of Truth,'* to us to abide in us because He will not leave us as orphans. Even so, He says He the Spirit of Truth would abide in us and He, Jesus, would be in us; this is clearly a picture of the tri-unity of the Godhead. [100] The Holy Spirit will pray through us because we don't know how to pray like we should, and sometimes the burden we have is too much to express. [101] As previously noted, Jesus has said that the Father would give us another Helper, and He also says, "I will come to you." This also implies that The Father, Jesus and The Holy Spirit are one. Also note the Holy Spirit will live with us and be in us and Jesus said I will come to you; here we have another concept of the Trinity. *After a little while the world will no longer see Me, but you will see Me; because I live, you will live also. In that day you will know I am in My Father, and you in Me, and I in you."* [102] Jesus said that if we believed in Him, the Spirit whom He would send would be as it were rivers of water flowing from our belly, but that would be after He had been glorified. [103] Notice Jesus said 'The Helper;' the being a definite article that describes Him as an individual or a distinct personality.

The Holy Spirit **Convicts of Sin** and **He calls** and **separates** those for ministry. Jesus told His disciples if He didn't go away He could not send the Holy Spirit, but if He goes He will send Him and *'He **will convict the world of concerning sin and righteousness and judgment**: concerning* *sin, because they do not believe in Me; and concerning righteousness, because I go to the Father, and you no longer see Me; and concerning judgment, because the ruler of this world has been judged.'* [104] The Holy Spirit appoints certain people for His ministry. *"Set apart for 'ME' Barnabas and Saul for the work to which I have called them."* [105]

The Holy Spirit **sanctifies the believer.** [106] The word sanctify means to 'set apart' for a sacred purpose.

The Holy Spirit **regenerates.** *"He saved us, not on the basis of deeds which we had done in righteousness, but according to His mercy by the* **washing of regeneration** *and renewing of* **the Holy Spirit***, whom HE poured out upon us richly through Jesus Christ our Savior."* [107]

He draws us to God for Salvation. *"The Spirit and the bride say, "Come." And let the one who hears say, "Come." And let the one who is thirsty come; let the one who wishes take the water of life without cost."* [108]

The Spirit **Bestows of the Power of God on believers**. *"My message and my preaching were not with wise and persuasive words, but with a* **demonstration of the Spirit's power**, *so that your faith might not rest on men's wisdom, but on God's power."* [109] Again, we see here that The Holy Spirit is a distinct personality and also part of the Godhead. Holy Ghost/Spirit is from the Greek word *pneuma* which means a *current* of air, i.e. *breath (blast)* or a *breeze*; by analogy or figurative *a spirit*, it can also be used of the human rational *soul*, it also by implication means origin or mental *disposition*, etc. It could also be used in connection with an angel, or (divine) God, Christ's *Spirit*, the Holy *Spirit* also translated- ghost, life, spirit (-ual, -ually) and/or mind. But in all of the previous references it is rendered *God* or *the Holy*. [110]

The word Trinity is not mentioned in the Bible. Generally speaking most Jewish people do not believe in the concept of the Trinity. However, noting the above Scriptures there are three distinct personalities or essences of God, yet Scripture states God is one.

Chapter Three

[1] 2 Chronicles 20:6, Hebrews 1:3, and Colossians 1:17, Proverbs 19:21 & 21:31, Romans 9:19-20, Psalm 33:10-11
[2] Genesis 1:1
[3] Isaiah 41:14
[4] 2 Chronicles 20:6
[5] Exodus 3:14-15
[6] Isaiah 44:6
[7] Genesis 21:33
[8] Daniel 7:9, 13, 22
[9] Deuteronomy 32:35-36
[10] Genesis 25:25-26
[11] Isaiah 9:6
[12] Psalm 78:35
[13] Deuteronomy 32:39
[14] Psalm 99:4
[15] Genesis 25:25-26
[16] #6117[6]
[17] # 3068[6]
[18] Genesis 1:1
[19] Genesis 1:26
[20] John 17:20-21
[21] John 1:1-2
[22] Matthew 3:13-17
[23] Genesis 14:10-20
[24] #'s 410, 5928, 5945[6]
[25] Luke 2:14
[26] Genesis 14:22
[27] Daniel 12:7
[28] Exodus 3:14
[29] http://www.jewfaq.org/alephbet.htm
[30] http://en.wikipedia.org/wiki/English_alphabet
[31] #3068-Genesis 17:1 & 49:24, #7703[6]
[32] Revelation 19:6
[33] Psalm 139:7-12
[34] Psalm 139:11
[35] Psalm 44:21b
[36] Psalm 139: 1-4

Christianity

[37] Leviticus 10:3, [8] The word 'holy' according to Webster's means 'to be set apart to the service of God or a god: SACRED OR characterized by perfection and transcendence: commanding absolute adoration and reverence <the ~ Lord God Almighty>.
[38] Exodus 19:22
[39] Leviticus 21:6
[40] Isaiah 52:10, Ephesians 1:20, Hebrews 1:3
[41] Exodus 20:3, 7
[42] Exodus 15:3
[43] Exodus 34:6; Psalm 37:26, 1 Chronicles 16:34, Psalm 57:3, Psalm 100:5, #'s 2617 &7356 from OT-Hebrew and # 1656 NT-Greek
[44] Exodus 33:19; Jonah 4:2; 1 Peter 2:3, # 2580 OT-Hebrew and #5485 NT-Greek
[45] Romans 5:17; Ephesians 1:7, James 4:6; 2 Corinthians 3:14,
[46] Hebrews 1:2
[47] Hebrews 1:3, Colossians 1:16-17
[48] Exodus 34:7
[49] Exodus 3:14-15, Psalm 68:4, the original word is YAH- I Am that I Am http://www.ancient-hebrew.org/28_chart.html , http://godwords.org/516/what-does-jesus-mean/ as well as many other sources.
[50] Hebrews 1:2
[51] Hebrews 1:3
[52] Hebrews 1:3
[53] Hebrew 7:26-27
[54] Hebrews 1:3
[55] Hebrews 1:8
[56] Psalm 45:7, pg 834
[57] Hebrews 1:9
[58] John 1:14
[59] Colossians 2:9
[60] John 16: 28,
[61] John 16:15a
[62] John 8:58
[63] John 6:35
[64] John 8:12
[65] John 8:23
[66] John 10:9
[67] John 10:11
[68] John 11:25
[69] John 14: 6
[70] Isaiah 9:6
[71] John 1:1-2

God, Who is He?

[72] John 1:3-4
[73] John 4:14
[74] Galatians 1:3-4
[75] Revelation 5:9
[76] Hebrews 2:17
[77] Hebrews 3:1
[78] Isaiah 63:16
[79] Revelation 19:16,
[80] Revelation 22:16
[81] Matthew 1:23,
[82] 1 Corinthians 10:4
[83] Romans 11:26
[84] John 15:14
[85] James 4:12,
[86] Colossians 1:27, 1 Timothy 1:1
[87] John 5:26, 27
[88] 1 John 3: 8, Hebrews 2:14-15, Colossians 2:15
[89] Galatians 4:4-5
[90] John 1:29
[91] Luke 1:32-33
[92] Revelations 19:11-13, 16
[93] Matthew 28:19-20 [8]
[94] John 3:16
[95] Matthew 1:18 & Genesis 1:2
[96] John 16:7
[97] John 16:13-15
[98] John 16:15
[99] John 14:26 [8]
[100] John 14:15-18 [4]
[101] Romans 8:26 [4]
[102] John 14:19-20 [4]
[103] John 7:38-39
[104] John 16:7-12
[105] Acts 13:2
[106] Romans 15:16
[107] Titus 3:5-6
[108] Revelation 22:17
[109] 1 Corinthians 2:4-5
[110] #4151 [6]

Chapter Four

Creation of Man

In order to understand the need for Christianity, we need to understand man's original created state, and why we are not living in that state at the present time.

Mans Original State

God said, "Let US make man (ad-dahm) – human kind. In Our image, according to Our likeness; *LET* US –vs: 26 us . . . Our . . . Our[1]. image . . . likeness. [2] Man was *made* rather than being spoken into existence as all of the rest of creation and the other creatures on the earth were. The word 'make' *-aw-saw'-to* do or make, in the broadest sense and widest application it means to accomplish, bring forth, exercise, and fashion; [3] which are but a few of the words translated from this Hebrew word. The word *in,* in the above text is used as a *function* word to indicate *the same nature of.* [4] God said let Us (God the Father, Son and Holy Spirit) make man of the same nature We have. **Image** means a *reproduction or imitation of the form of a person or thing*, 'according' [5] to Our likeness...." **Likeness** means *the quality or state of being like, appearance, resemblance, semblance, copy, etc.* [6] So God made us with His nature and appearance. We were a copy, semblance of or like Him not only in appearance but like HIM-plural or with a plural nature. The characteristics of God the Father, God the Son and the Holy Spirit were mans originally **less the deity**. How can I say we are plural? We were created with a body, God breathed into us the breath of life and we became a living soul, and we were as it was 'filled' with the Spirit of God in the inner man. To further explain this concept, your *body* will 'tell' you or show you a thing such as it is hungry, thirsty, tired, etc.

Your *soul* which is your mind and will and emotions also conceptually 'tell' you things such desires, yearnings, wants, and moods. It will also 'tell' you intellectual things, where reasoning may come into play. The *spirit* will also 'tell' you things, instructing what is right or wrong. Some call this a sixth sense, intuition; conscience. It can as well perceive metaphysical presence etc. *"The man and his wife were both naked, and they felt no shame."* [7] It is apparent man did not use the power of reasoning concerning God or His commands until it was introduced in the Garden when the serpent questioned God's command to Eve. The NLT translates in Genesis 3:8 this way. *"The woman was convinced."*

CREATION OF ADAM

Adam – ***Adamah*** means red or earth, hence the name given to the first man, **Ad-dahm** – Hebrew word for Adam means *human kind made from the earth*. Genesis 2:7, 8: *"He breathed into his nostrils the breath of life and he became **a living soul**."* Notice God created everything else by His Word but man was different. First **He formed** him; the Hand of the Almighty God according to the Hebrew means *He squeezed him into shape, molded him as a potter, He fashioned him*, then **He breathed** life into him and he ***became*** a living **soul**; the face of Almighty God in the face of man. The Hebrew word for breathed is **neshamah** [8] which means God literally puffed wind into Adams nostrils— the breath of life; not only wind but also inspiration, his soul and spirit. The Hebrew word for soul **nephesh** [9] means basically your mind, will and emotions including appetite. *So your SOUL is*–**Mind, Will, Emotions.** "Image" includes such characteristics as "righteousness and holiness," [10] and "knowledge." [11] Believers are to be "conformed to the likeness" of Christ, [12] and will someday be "like Him" [13] and rule. Man is the climax of God's creative activity, and God has "crowned him with glory and honor" and "made him ruler" over the rest of His creation. [14] "Since man was created in the image of the divine King, *delegated sovereignty (kingship) was bestowed on him.* The New Testament also shows man was made in the image and likeness of God. [15]

CREATION OF EVE

Now, '*but for Adam there was not found a **helper** (**KJV-help meet**) comparable to him,* so God **made** the woman and brought her to Adam. [16] The Hebrew word for '*help meet*' is **ezar** *–ay'-zer- aid and comes from the prim root azar –**aw-zer'**- to surround, i.e. protect, aid: help, succor;* [17] 'succor is defined in Webster's as -run to help, something that furnishes relief, aid. The Hebrew word for *made* is **banah**- *baw-naw'*–which comes *from the prim root* t*o build.*[18] So by definition a woman was created to be a wife, a helpmeet, to surround her husband with aid, to run to help him, to protect him and she is to obtain children for him. As I saw this word protect, I said, "Lord, I thought man was to protect his wife, how are we supposed to protect our husbands, since we are deemed the weaker vessel?" This is what I heard in my spirit: "A wife is to protect her husband's integrity in the community and home by revering him before her children and others and take care of his emotional and physical needs from the desire to go after other women whether visual or physical."

"<u>Therefore</u> the man is to **leave** his father and mother and **cleave** (**KJV**) *to his wife and they shall become* **one** *flesh"*.[19] **Cleave** in the Hebrew is "**dabaq** – *daw-bak'* which means to impinge (to fasten or drive in), i.e. cling or adhere; figuratively to catch by pursuit:-abide fast, cleave (fast together), follow close (hard after), be joined (together), keep (fast), overtake, pursue hard, stick, take.[20] So man is to follow close or hard after his wife, to catch her by pursuit, abide fast, cling and adhere to her; to literally overtake her.

Now, let's look at the word '<u>Therefore</u>' at the beginning of this verse. It draws attention to the previous verse. In essences what Scripture is saying: ***The reason man is to leave his father and mother and cleave to his wife is because she was taken out of man and she is to be flesh of his flesh, or they are to be one flesh.*** We have a tendency to look at this as just a physical union. However by definition of the Hebrew word for 'flesh' – ***basar*** means, *body or person*, the primary root word meaning *to be fresh i.e. full*, [21] it implies when man and woman are joined they become a whole or complete person. As if by implication man received part of the characteristics of the Godhead and woman received other parts of the characteristics. They were to be one and co-rule as one.

MAN AND WOMAN'S PLACE IN CREATION

"Then He (God) said: 'let' <u>them</u> *have dominion over....."*[22] (Basically everything on earth and immediate heaven.) '*Multiply*' – i.e. obtain children, *'and fill the earth'* with them, then He says, *'and* <u>***subdue***</u> <u>***it***</u>*: have dominion over'* [23]... ***Subdue*** in Hebrew is kabash- *kaw-bash'* – *to tread down, negative sense-disregard,* <u>*positive sense-to conquer, subjugate*</u>, and violate: <u>*bring into bondage, force, keep under, subdue, bring into subjection.*</u> ***Dominion*** in Hebrew *is radah i.e. raw-daw':* to tread down, i.e. to conquer, or *(specifically)* **to crumble off:** *(come to, make to)* have dominion, prevail against, reign, rule *(-r, over),* take. [24] **So Adam**

and Eve were to take control over the earth, to rule it, to subdue and bring into subjection any and all forces that were insubordinate to their authority. (Meditate on this particular statement for a moment). I reiterate that they were initially co-rulers. Remember they became *'one'* a complete or whole person when united; they were not vying for control over one another.

God said; *'**Let' them**...* have dominion
So we will look at the word *let*.

> Webster's defines let as, to give the opportunity to, ALLOW, PERMIT, *LET may imply a positive giving of permission* **but more often implies failure to prevent either through inadvertence or inattention and negligence or through lack of power of effective authority**. *(I will refer back to this last part of the definition later so remember it or make note so as to be able to refer back to it.)*

For all intents and purposes Adam and Eve were to co-rule and govern the earth and all its creatures. They were to bring into subjection any and all creatures that did not submit to their authority. They were to dominate the earth. After the 'fall,' part of the curse for Eve was to be subject to her husbands' authority. Your desire will be 'to rule over' your husband, but he shall rule over you. Because Eve was deceived by the serpent and inadvertently did not subdue him, she is to be subject to her husband's authority. Adam not being deceived and yet not subduing the serpent is the one through whom all sin is passed. This will be clearly understood when we look at Cain and Abel in a following chapter.

CHAPTER FOUR

[1] Genesis 3:22; 11:7; Isaiah 6:8; see also 1Kings 22:19-23; Job 15:8; Jeremiah 23:18
[2] Genesis 1:26
[3] # 6213[6]
[4] Webster's defines 'in' according as-*in conformity with.* pg 421[7]
[5] Webster's Dictionary, pg 415[7]
[6] Webster's Dictionary, pg 489[7]
[7] Genesis 2:25
[8] # 5301- nesh-aw-maw': a puff, i.e. wind angry or vital breath, divine inspiration, intellect. Breath (eth) inspiration, soul, spirit.[6]
[9] # 5315 neh'-fesh: prim root-to be breath, to breathe upon, refreshed. Properly a breathing creature, i.e. animal (abstr.) vitality; used very widely in a literal, accommodated or figurative sense (**bodily or mental**):-any, **appetite**, beast, body, breath, creatures, life, **lust,** man, me, **mind**, mortally, one, own, person, **pleasure**, (her-, him-, my-, thy-) self, them (your) selves,+ slay, **soul**, + tablet, they, thing,(X she) **will**, X would have it.)[6]
[10] Ephesians 4:24
[11] Colossians 3:10
[12] Romans 8:29
[13] 1 John 3:2
[14] Genesis 1:26-28, Genesis 5:1 and 9:6, Psalm 8:5-8
[15] 1 Corinthians 11:7, James 3:9
[16] Genesis 2:18-22
[17] #5826 & 5828[6]
[18] #1129 *(lit & fig): begin to)* build *(-er)* obtain children, make, repair, set (up). X surely. (The X means it's an added certainty.)[6]
[19] Genesis 2:24
[20] #1692[6]
[21] #1320[6]
[22] Genesis 1:28
[23] Genesis 1:28
[24] #3533[6]

CHAPTER FIVE

SATAN

WHAT HE WAS, WHO HE IS, WHAT HE DOES AND HIS ULTIMATE END!

According to the Naves Topical Bible the name 'Satan,' from the Greek and Hebrew definitions is 'a hostile opponent.' Defined in Webster's Dictionary is a fiend, the spirit of evil, diabolical and enemy of God. [1] From the Webster's' Bible Dictionary, Satan is defined as an enemy or adversary or the chief of fallen spirits, an enemy of God and man. [2] In the Bible he is shown to be hostile to everything good and was thrown to the earth. [3]

Satan is the prince and power over the air surrounding the immediate heavens over the earth, chief ruler of demons and wicked persons. [4]

Satan is the father of deception. Paul in speaking to Elymas a sorcerer makes this statement: *"You are a **child of the devil** and **an enemy of everything that is right**, you are full of all kinds of deceit and trickery. Will you never stop perverting the right ways of the Lord?"* [5]

Satan is still subject to God and can do nothing but what God permits as seen in Job[6] and in the New Testament Jesus is talking to Simon Peter about his denial of knowing Him: *"Simon, Simon, Satan has asked to sift you as wheat."*[7] Note Satan had to ask to sift Peter.

Satan is evil. How he came into existence is not expressly written but because John 1:3 says; *"Through Him (Jesus Christ) <u>all things were made</u> and <u>without Him (Jesus Christ)</u> **nothing** <u>was made that has been made</u>."*[5] We can rest assured that Satan was created by God through Jesus Christ for His purpose. Jesus said in Revelation that he (Satan) was cast down to the earth, the following Scriptures have been attributed as a description of that fall and the reason.

"How you have fallen from heaven, O star of the morning, son of the dawn!
You have been cut down to the earth, you who have weakened the nations!
"But you said in your heart, 'I will ascend to heaven;
I will raise my throne above the stars of God,
And I will sit on the mount of assembly
in the recesses of the north.
'I will ascend above the heights of the clouds;
I will make myself like the Most High." [8]
And again: *"Son of man, take up a lament concerning the king of Tyre and say to him: 'This is what the Sovereign LORD says:*
'You were the model of perfection, full of wisdom and perfect in beauty.
You were in Eden, the garden of God;
every precious stone adorned you: ruby, topaz and emerald,
chrysolite, onyx and jasper, sapphire, turquoise and beryl.
Your settings and mountings were made of gold;
on the day you were created they were prepared.
You were anointed as a guardian cherub, for so I ordained you.
You were on the holy mount of God; you walked among the fiery stones.
You were blameless in your ways <u>from the day you were created</u> till wickedness was found in you." [9]

Jesus made this statement in Luke 10:18: *He (Jesus) replied, "I saw Satan fall like lightning from heaven."*[5]

Satan is under judgment as we see in Timothy in reference to appointing deacons: *"not a new convert, so that he will not become conceited and fall into the condemnation by the devil."* [10] Although he is the ruler of a powerful kingdom in opposition to God as stated in Matthew and Luke [11] he is never-the-less still subject to God. Because he hates God; he hates man because man was made in the image of God, he desires nothing better than to defeat God's plan of grace toward man. [12] He steals the Word from the heart of man, [13] and causes spiritual blindness, [14] and physical infirmities [sickness and disease]. [15] The devices of Satan are listed in 2 Corinthians 2:11 and 12:7; Ephesians 6:11-12 & 16; 1 Thessalonians 2:18; and 1Timothy 3:6-7, never-the-less he **was** defeated by Christ at Calvary. [16] Any and all power he now holds sway over mankind is due to man's sin and rebellion against God and a lack of belief concerning the truth of Scripture; that the purposes and plans of God will be fulfilled.

What is his end? *"And **He laid hold the dragon, that old serpent, which is the Devil, and Satan, and bound him a thousand years,** And **cast him into the bottomless pit, and shut him up,** and set a seal upon him, that he should deceive the nations no more, till the thousand years should be fulfilled......... And when the thousand years are expired, Satan shall be loosed out of his prison, And shall go out and deceive the nations which are in the four quarters of the earth......... And the devil that deceived them **was cast into the lake of fire and brimstone,** where the beast and the false prophet are, **and shall be tormented day and night <u>for ever and ever</u>."* [17]

Numerous times he is mentioned in regard to different events such as: Hymenaeus and Alexander delivered to,[18] he contends with Michael,[19] and his ministers masquerade as apostles of Christ.[20] He is to be resisted. [21] Resistance of him is effectual. [22] We have gracious deliverance from his power. [23] He persecutes the church. [24] Christ is accused of being him, [25] Paul accuses Elymas the sorcerer of being from him. [26] He is called: Beelzebub, [27] Belial, [28] the devil, [29] Satan, [30] Possibly Apollyon, [31] and Lucifer. [32]

CHAPTER FIVE

[1] Page 329[7]
[2] Page 700 [13]
[3] Revelation 12:7-9
[4] Ephesians 2:2
[5] Acts 13:10 [5]
[6] Job 1:6-12
[7] Luke 22:31[5]
[8] Isaiah 14:12-14[4]
[9] Ezekiel 28:12-28[5]
[10] 1Timothy 3:6[4]
[11] Matthew 12:26 & Luke 11:18
[12] 1 Peter 5:8
[13] Matthew 13:19, 38-39; Mark 4:15; Luke 8:12
[14] 2 Corinthians 4:4
[15] Luke 13:16
[16] Genesis 3:15; John 3:8
[17] Revelation 20:2, 3,7,10
[18] 1Timothy 1:20
[19] Jude 9
[20] 2Corinthians 11:15
[21] Ephesians 4:27, James 4:7; 1Peter 5:8-9
[22] 1John 2:13; 5:18
[23] Acts 27:18; Colossians 1:13
[24] Revelation 2:10, 13-14
[25] Matthew 9:34; Mark 2:22-26; Luke 11:15, 18
[26] Acts 13:10
[27] Matthew 12:24; Mark 3:22; Luke 11:15
[28] 2Corinthians 6:15
[29] Matthew 4:1; 13:39; Luke 4:2-6; Revelation 20:2
[30] 1Chronicles 21:1; Job 1:6; Zechariah 3:1; Luke 22:31; John 13:27; Acts 5:3; 26:18; Romans 16:20
[31] Revelation 9:11
   [32] Isaiah 14:12

Chapter Six

The Garden of Eden
and THE FALL

❦

'*Now the LORD God had planted a garden in the east, in Eden; and there He put the man He had formed. And the LORD God made all kinds of trees grow out of the ground—trees that were pleasing to the eye and good for food. In the middle of the garden were* **the tree of life** *and* **the tree of the knowledge of good and evil**.' [1] '*The LORD God* <u>**commanded**</u> *the man, saying, "From any tree of the garden you may eat freely,* <u>but</u> *from the* **tree of the knowledge of good and evil** *you shall not eat, for in the day that you eat from it you will surely die."* [2] '*And the man and his wife were both naked and were not embarrassed or ashamed in each other's presence.' NOW the serpent was more subtle and crafty than any living creature of the field which the Lord God had made. And he [the serpent] said to the woman, "Can it really be that God has said, 'You shall not eat from every tree of the garden?'" And the woman said to the serpent, "We may eat the fruit from the trees of the garden, except the fruit from the tree which is in the middle of the garden. God has said, 'You shall not eat of it, neither shall you touch it, lest you die.'" But the serpent said to the woman, "You shall not surely die, for God knows that in the day you eat of it your eyes will be opened, and you will be like God, knowing the difference between good and evil and blessing and calamity." And when the woman saw that the* **tree was good** *(suitable and pleasant)* **for food** *and that it was* **delightful to look at***, and a tree to be* **desired in order to make one wise***, she took of its fruit and ate; and she gave some also to her husband, and he ate. Then the eyes of them both were opened,*

Christianity

and they knew that they were naked; and they sewed fig leaves together and made themselves apron like girdles. And they heard the sound of the Lord God walking in the garden in the cool of the day, and Adam and his wife hid themselves from the presence of the Lord God among the trees of the garden. But the Lord God called to Adam and said to him, "Where are you?" He said, I heard the sound of You [walking] in the garden, and I was afraid because I was naked; and I hid myself. And He said, "Who told you that you were naked? Have you eaten of the tree of which I commanded you that you should not eat?" And the man said, "The woman whom You gave to be with me—she gave me [fruit] from the tree, and I ate."[3]

There are several things that I want to point out in this portion of scripture, first: God had commanded them not to eat from the *'tree of the knowledge of good and evil'* stating that they would surely die upon doing so. As we well know they did not physically die at this point. What happened? All of a sudden they knew they were naked. Why or how? I believe because they were created in the image and likeness of God, they were originally clothed or filled with the glory of God and because they were created in His likeness, He is Spirit – the Spirit was in them or on them and the Glory or Spirit of the Lord departed from them. Also I want to point out that Eve added to the Word of the Lord (*neither shall ye touch it*). It also says "*their eyes were opened*,' because we know they could physically see it had to be the eyes of their understanding (they *knew*), so before partaking of the fruit they were totally unaware of evil, they did not have the ability to perceive nor reason between good and evil (*which implies complete innocence*). Hence, 'reason' was introduced at this point. Regardless, Ephesians 2:1 says, *"And you He made alive, who were dead in trespasses and sins."*[8] Implying before our new birth in Christ we were dead. So in essence they had died in some way. To my understanding the Spirit of the Lord or Glory of the Lord departed,[4] leaving them empty or dead inside, feeling EXPOSED, hence the need to hide from God. They did not immediately physically die but by eating of the fruit of *'the Knowledge of Good and Evil'* instead of *'The Tree of Life'* they had sealed their fate to physical death. *Then the LORD God said, "Behold, the man has become like one of Us,* **knowing** *good and evil; and now, he might stretch out his hand, and take also from the tree of life, and eat, and live forever"— therefore the LORD God sent him out from the garden of Eden, to cultivate the ground from which he was taken. So He drove the man out; and at the east of the garden of Eden He* (God) *stationed the cherubim and the flaming sword which turned every direction to guard the way to the tree of life."*[5] Because of these verses, I believe man was created to remain in a state of complete and perpetual innocence living forever on the earth. Had Adam or Eve for that matter, **subdued** the serpent at the point of temptation and instead eaten from the *'Tree of Life'* there would be no sin and we would live forever in a state of perpetual innocence. Notice to the extended hyphen at the end of verse 22 (which is not in some translations), it's almost as if the thought of what would occur should they eat of 'the tree of life' in this *awakened state* would be too much for even God to contemplate or express.

Also remember that God had said for Adam and Eve to **have dominion** over all the earth and **subdue** it. *"When the woman saw* (awakening of reason) *that the fruit of the tree was good for food and pleasing to the eye, and also desirable for gaining wisdom, she took some and ate it. She also gave some to her husband <u>who was with her</u>."*[6] *"The woman was convinced!"* Eve was deceived or tricked, into partaking of the fruit.[7] Don't forget about the words *'dominion'* and *'subdue'* or the word *'let'*; I will explain these three words in the next chapter in detail. It is crucial for you keep this in mind. Now look back at Genesis chapter 3:13-15. *"Then the LORD God said to the woman, "What is this you have done?" The woman said,* **"The serpent deceived me**, *and I ate." So the LORD God said to the serpent, "Because you have done this, cursed are you above all the livestock and all the wild animals! You will crawl on your belly and you will eat dust all the days of your life. And I will put enmity between you and the woman, and between your offspring and hers;* **he will crush your head, and you will strike his heel**.*"* Because the serpent deceived her, he was cursed with being the only above ground land animal without feet and legs. But more importantly in verse 15; the 'offspring' it refers to a singular person in both instances. It does not say 'they' will crush your head and 'you all,' or 'all of you' will strike 'their heels,' but in relation to both it is singular. This is very important in understanding who the 'He' is and who the 'you' is. Jesus Christ is the 'He' and Satan is the 'you.' 'He,' Jesus will crush 'your,' Satan's head. Crush means to pulverize or to completely destroy. Remember Satan is the opponent of God, Christ, Holy Spirit and man (because we were created in the image of God). As you study these definitions within the context of the Scripture you will begin to see in Genesis 3:6 that Eve was deceived and neither she nor Adam 'subdued' the serpent. Remember the italicized part of the definition of *'let'* in the previous chapter. I included it because of the role of Satan in the Garden. God had given Adam and Eve the governing authority over the earth[8] and had warned them not to eat of the fruit of the Tree of the Knowledge of Good and Evil.[9] Had Adam or Eve for that matter taken the initiative and

SUBDUED the serpent upon his audacity to suggest God was a liar, the fall would not have taken place. They had ample opportunity to subdue Satan through the serpent in the Garden, but they **neglected** to do it. So (here the word *let* comes into play): ***They had failed through*** *inadvertence and negligence* ***to prevent Satan from hindering God's command for them to have dominion over the earth. They did not use the authority God had given them to subdue the earth and all the spiritual forces within the earth's atmosphere.*** Read–Genesis 1:26-28. What were God's commands to Adam and Eve? *To have dominion and subdue the earth*! It was both a position and authority. Adam and Eve were, as it were, Gods ambassadors on the earth!

CHAPTER SIX

[1] Genesis 2: 8–9[5]
[2] Genesis 2:16-17[4]
[3] Genesis 2:25-3:12[1]
[4] see 1 Samuel 4:21-22[4]
[5] Genesis 3:22-24[8]
[6] Genesis 3:6[2]
[7] Genesis 3:13-15[5]
[8] Genesis 1:26
[9] Genesis 2:17

Chapter Seven

Sin

What is sin?

Using the next to last statement of the previous chapter, *sin is the inadvertence and negligence of obedience to God's commands either through willful rebellion, deception or lack of understanding of the power that has been invested in us.* Here's what Scripture has to say: '*As for you, you were dead in your transgressions and sins, in which you used to live __when you followed the ways of this world and the ruler of the kingdom of the air,__ the spirit who is now at work in those __who are disobedient__. All of us also lived among them at one time, __gratifying the cravings of our sinful nature and following its desires and thoughts__. __Like the rest, we were by nature objects of wrath__.*' [1] And '*Do not love the world or anything in the world. If __anyone loves the world__, the love of the Father is not in him. For everything in the world—__the cravings of sinful man, the lust of his eyes and the boasting of what he has and does__—comes not from the Father but from the world.*' [2] Basically, the act of sin is anything done independently of God and/or His known will, or in essence 'TO BE YOUR OWN GOD.' Satan fell from heaven because he wanted to lift himself above God or in essence be God. In Luke 10:18, *He* (Jesus) *replied, "I saw Satan fall like lightning from heaven."* Quoting Isaiah: *"How you have fallen from heaven, O star of the morning, son the dawn! You have been cut down to the earth, you who have weakened the nations! But you said in your heart, I will ascend to heaven; I will raise my throne above the stars of God; And I WILL SIT ON THE MOUNT OF ASSEMBLY, In the recesses of the north. I will ascend above the heights of the clouds; I WILL MAKE MYSELF LIKE THE MOST HIGH."* [3] Man has in essence done the same thing, i.e. "I did it my way," or the more recent, "It's all about me." What was Satan's statement to Eve? *'You will be like God.'* In Isaiah the word *iniquities* was used in place of the word *sin*. *"But your iniquities have made a separation between you and your God, and your sins have hidden His face from you, so that He does not hear."* [4] Iniquities-is defined in Webster as, gross injustice or wickedness, SIN. [5]

In studying Genesis and 'sin' in the Garden of Eden and also the account of Cain and Abel; SIN IS A LIVING ENTITY or A POWER or FORCE AT WORK IN THE WORLD. Let's look at the pronouncement of the curse God made on Eve in Genesis 3:16: *"I will greatly multiply your sorrow and your conception; in pain you shall bring forth children; Your desire shall be <u>for</u> your husband, and he shall rule over you."* I want to look at the word *'for'* or *'toward'* as it is written in the King James Version. The word *'for'* or *'toward'* has the connotation of 'ruling over' as we see in Genesis 4:7, where Cain slew Abel and God is talking to Cain about sin. *"If you do well, will you not be accepted? And if you do not do well, sin lies at the door. And its desire is <u>for</u> you, but you should rule over it."* In these verses *sin* and *it* are used as nouns, personifying sin. The word *lies* is translated from *rabats* [5] which also means to *'crouch'* or *'lurk.'* Notice <u>its</u> *'desire'* is *'for'* you. The exact same wording used in Genesis 3:16 speaking of Eve, "Your *'desire'* shall be *'for'* your husband..." God says to Cain, 'but you must *rule* over <u>it</u>,' and to Eve, 'he shall *rule* over you.'

The FALL was brought about by 'SIN'; *"Wherefore, as by one man (Adam) <u>sin</u> entered into the world, and death by sin, and so death passed upon all men, for that all have sinned."* [6] Note: Adam is ultimately the one to whom responsibility for sin in the earth has fallen. Eve was deceived (tricked-the same word magic comes from) while in the presence of Adam. [7] Again, this explains how Jesus could be born in human flesh and still be without sin; He was born of a virgin-woman. All sin as the above Scripture from Romans states was passed from 'man' Adam to every person. Only through the virgin birth could Christ be fully man and yet by conception of the Holy Spirit be fully God and not inherit the sin nature. Never-the-less the spirit of man died that day in the Garden of Eden, the counsel of God was no longer their daily bread-they had become estranged from Him-He sent them out to live independent of His daily counsel. By the 10th generation man had become so evil that God was sorry He had made man. God *'repented* (had a change of mind and heart) *that He had made man,' 'Then the LORD saw that the wickedness of man was great on the earth, and* that *every intent of the thoughts of his heart* was only evil continually. The LORD *was sorry* that He had made man on the earth, and He *was grieved* in His heart. The LORD said, "I will blot out man whom I have created from the face of the land, from man to animals to creeping things and to birds of the sky; *for I am sorry that I have made them.*" But *"Noah found favor in the eyes of the LORD"* [8] HE, GOD, destroyed every person except Noah and his wife and sons and sons' wives by flood. When Noah and his family left the ark, God gave Noah part of the command He had given Adam, '*Be fruitful, multiply and fill the earth.*' [9] Notice: God did not tell Noah to subdue the earth. **Satan by deception had gained control over the earth. He in essence stole, by deceit, the dominion over the earth.** As a result all creation is subject to corruption, [10] the corruption brought about by the evil intent of Satan which is to destroy everything God has created for His glory, praise and honor. [11]

Who sins? How do we know we have sinned?

As it is written "There is **no one** *righteous,* **not even one***; there is no one who understands, no one who seeks God.* **All have turned away***, they have together become worthless;* **there is no one who does good, not even one***. Their throats are open graves; their tongues practice deceit. The poison of vipers is on their lips. Their mouths are full of cursing and bitterness. Their feet are swift to shed blood; ruin and misery mark their ways, and the way of peace they do not know.* **There is no fear of God before their eyes**." [12]

"[But] *he who commits sin [who practices evildoing] is of the devil [takes his character from the evil one], for the devil has sinned (violated the divine law) from the beginning. The reason the Son of God was made manifest (visible) was to undo (destroy, loosen, and dissolve) the works the devil [has done]* " [13] "*for* **all have sinned** *and come short of the glory of God,....*" [14]

Let's look again at 1 John 2:16, *For all that is in the world—the* **lust of the flesh** *(good for food)* [craving for sensual gratification] *and the* **lust of the eyes** *(pleasant to the eyes)* [greedy longings of the mind] *and the* **pride of life** *(desirable to make one wise)* [assurance in one's own resources or in the stability of earthly things]—*these do not come from the Father but are from the world* [itself]. What did the serpent point out to Eve in the Garden? The fruit was good for food, pleasant to the eyes and desirable to make one wise. Let's look again at 1 John 2:17 in the Amplified Bible; "*And the world passes away and disappears, and with it the* **forbidden cravings** *(the passionate desires, the lust) of it; but he who does* *the will of God and carries out His purposes in his life abides (remains) forever."* Now let's look at Galatians 5:19-21; *"Now the doings (practices) of the flesh are clear (obvious): they are immorality, impurity, indecency, Idolatry, sorcery, enmity, strife, jealousy, anger (ill temper), selfishness, divisions (dissensions), party spirit, factions (sects with peculiar opinions, heresies), Envy, drunkenness, carousing, and the like. I warn you beforehand, just as I did previously,* **that those who do such things shall not inherit the kingdom of God."**

So we see here that '**sin**' is lust of the flesh, lust of the eyes and pride. Lust is covetousness, the ninth commandment states 'Thou shalt not covet.'[15] Every sin, whether hidden, overt, known or unknown, flows from these three things. Lust is an intense craving or desiring what one does not have. Lust of the eyes is looking with longing at something, whether it is food, material possessions, or a person. It encompasses the imagination. Lust of the flesh is anything that gratifies the physical body. It too may be food, material possession or persons, it is anything sensual. Remember sin was related as a power or entity working within us through lust and/or pride. Pride is arrogance, conceit, smugness and/or self-importance. Just last evening I was studying on the sin of pride. As I meditated and prayed, God began to show me that if I complain it is because of pride, either someone or something is not living or being what I feel I deserve and I am exalting myself in saying it's not good enough for me. If I shrink back or withhold myself from another person, that's pride, in essence I'm relaying that they are not performing to my standard or they are not worth my attention. If I refuse to humble myself before God and pray, that's pride, because I cannot approach God without humbling myself. The very essence of pride says I'm more important or what I want is more important than anyone or anything else. It is self- exaltation or independence above or of God. 'It's all about me.' What is the middle letter of the word sin? **I**. So sin is, in essence, 'being your own god'!

What are the consequences of sin?

Curses are the consequence of sin. *"However, if you do not obey the LORD your God and do not carefully follow all his commands and decrees I am giving you today,* **all these curses will come** *upon you and overtake you:"* [16] You will find all the curses in the continuation of that Scripture. "A curse is essentially a divine judgment. A curse may be uttered as a solemn oath, warning of what God will do if His covenant is violated. A curse may also be the judgment itself, spoken of after it has been imposed. Such a curse binds and limits its object. It brings about diminished circumstances that stand in contrast to the blessing God yearns to provide." [17] I will add that the curse of sin, i.e. sickness, disease, confusion, anxiety, etc.: its consequences (ultimately-death) are still in effect just as sin is still in effect. When we sin, we invite judgment and come under a curse. The effects of sin are passed from generation to generation through the father all the way from Adam. Curses of sin are passed down three to four generations. [18] A bastard curse is affected to the tenth generation. [19] It is the LORD who pronounces the blessings and the LORD that curses. There are times when an angel of the LORD will pronounce a curse such as in Judges 5:23. "*The LORD shall send upon thee cursing, vexation, and rebuke......The LORD shall make the pestilence cleave unto thee.........The LORD shall smite thee with a consumption and with a fever and with an inflammation, and with extreme burning...*" [20]

What is the result of sin?
"*For the wages of sin is death,*" [21] Sin breeds death, "*You will surely die,*" [22] "*But he who **misses*** *Me or sins against Me **wrongs and injures himself**; all who hate Me **love and court death**.*" [23] "*For many walk, of whom I have told you often, and now tell you even weeping, that they are the enemies of the cross of Christ: **whose end is destruction,** whose god is their belly, and whose glory is **their shame**—who mind earthly things.*" [24] "*If any man teach otherwise and consent not to wholesome words, even the words of our Lord Jesus Christ, and to the doctrine which is according to godliness, he is proud, knowing nothing, but doting about questions and strifes of words, where of cometh envy, strife, railings, evil surmisings, Perverse disputings of men of corrupt minds and destitute of the truth, supposing that gain is godliness: from such withdraw thyself.*"[25] **We see here those who sin are destitute of the truth and have corrupt minds,** and in the New King James version it states; **they wrong and injure themselves and they court death**. Those who sin are hostile to God and do not submit to Him. [26] Those who sin, lack wisdom and understanding and are destroying their own lives, [27] and in the end will be judged according to their works. [87] They will be cast into the lake of fire and be tormented day and night forever. [29] Revelation gives examples of sins "*but the **cowardly, unbelieving, abominable, murderers, sexually immoral, sorcerers, idolaters,** and **all liars** shall have their part in the lake which burns with fire* and brimstone, which is the second death."[30] **Ultimately for those who sin the consequence is hell. Their ultimate end will be burning in the lake of fire for all eternity with their father the devil. They are condemned.**

How can we escape the destruction of the force of sin in our lives? And how do we escape its consequences? Salvation! What is Salvation? What must I do to be 'saved'?

CHAPTER SEVEN

[1] Ephesians 2:1-3
[2] 1John 2:15-16
[3] Isaiah 14:12-14
[4] Isaiah 59: 2
[5] #7257
[6] Romans 5:12
[7] Genesis 3:6
[8] Genesis 6:5-8
[9] Genesis 9:1
[10] Romans 8:21-22
[11] Revelation 4:11
[12] Romans 3:10-18
[13] 1 John 3:8
[14] Romans 3:23
[15] Exodus 20:17
[16] Deuteronomy 28:15
[17] New Encyclopedia of Biblical Words
[18] Exodus 34:7
[19] Deuteronomy 23:2
[20] Deuteronomy 28:20-22
[21] Romans 6:23
[22] Genesis 2:17b
[23] Proverbs 8:36*(one of the definitions of sin from the original Greek word *Hamartia* means to miss the mark and not share in the prize.)
[24] Philippians 3:18-19
[25] 1Timothy 6:3-5
[26] Romans 8:7
[27] Proverbs 6:32
[28] Revelation 20:12-15
[29] Revelation 14:10-11
[30] Revelation 21:8

Chapter Eight

Salvation, Redemption

What is Salvation?

The Old Testament word *salvation* means to be delivered, rescued, victory, aid, health, and safe or safety and prosperity.[1] The New Testament word means basically the same except it includes the deliverer being God or Christ; it also has the connotation of liberation, being made whole, body, soul and spirit, deliverance, health, to be open-wide or free, to be safe, freedom, rescue, victory.[2] God, in His great mercy, not willing that anyone should perish, i.e. be separated from Him or go to hell, sent His only begotten Son into the world that through Him we might be saved.[3] Jesus Christ, God's own Son, is the true Light to show men to God. He came into the world He made, yet those in the world did not know him nor receive Him as their Savior, but to those who did trust Him to save them from sin, He gave the right, authority and power to become the children of God by His own will.[4]

In order to be saved, one must be born again.[5] To be born again one must come to the realization that he is lost, without hope and has no power within to provide Salvation. We are born as flesh and flesh cannot inherit the kingdom of God.[6] To inherit the kingdom of God one must be born of the Spirit.[7] Only God can provide the way and the means for our Salvation, and He did that through Jesus Christ. *"For God so loved the world, that He gave His only begotten Son, that **whoever believes in Him** shall not perish, but have eternal life. For God did not send the Son into the world to judge the world, but that the world might be saved through Him. He who believes in Him is not judged; he who does not believe has* *been judged already, because he has not believed in the name of the only begotten Son of God.*[8] Make note of the words '*in Him*' in the above Scriptures. 'In' is a preposition indicating a present relation to a condition; it is not just an acknowledgment of who God is or what He did. It is a trust in, adherence to, relying on and cleaving to God and Jesus Christ for eternal salvation.

Redemption

In the Old Testament the concept of redemption is played out through the deliverance of the children of Israel. God redeemed the children of Israel many times after they had been brought under the power of foreign kings. Redeem means to tear loose, to buy back, ransom, to release, deliver or avenge, it was usually by a next of or near kin, it denotes the relationship of those redeemed.[9] The same is true in the New Testament, however it is further carried out to mean ransom in full, riddance and Salvation.[10] Redemption is deliverance from the enslavement of sin (to be torn loose from sin) and release to a new freedom by the sacrifice of the Redeemer, Jesus Christ. The death of Christ is the redemptive price. The word contains both the ideas of deliverance and the price of that deliverance, or ransom. We are torn loose from our old sin nature; it has been buried with Christ in the waters of Baptism and He has raised us from the dead and given us new life in the Holy Spirit.

Becoming His Child, Adoption into Christ

"*But as many as received Him, to them He gave the* **right to become** *the children of God, to those who believe in His name.*"[11] Lets break down the phrase '*right to become*'. Right as a noun, according to Encarta Dictionary is: 'the entitlement or freedom or claim to property.' The King James Version says He gave us the *power* to become. The Amplified says it this way: "*But to as many as did receive and welcome Him, He gave the authority (power, privilege, right) to become the children of God, that is, to those who believe in (adhere to, trust in, and rely on) His name.*" So we were given the authority, power, privilege or right to become. When we '*receive*' Him, He gives us the right! The Bible has explicit instruction of how that 'right' is expressed (or evident) in our lives. It also says to '*become*' which according to Webster's Dictionary and Strong's Commentary means—to come into existence, to come to be, **to undergo change or development**. In Romans chapter eight Paul talks about walking after the Spirit and not after the flesh, "**For as many as <u>are led</u> by the Spirit of God, <u>they are the sons of God</u>.** *For ye have not received the*

Salvation, Redemption

spirit of bondage again to fear, but ye have received the Spirit of adoption, whereby we cry, Abba, Father." [12] In Galatians Paul makes this statement, *'But when the fullness of the time was come, God sent forth His Son, made of a woman, made under the law, to redeem them that were under who the law,* **that we might receive the adoption of sons.***'* [13] We **might** – the power, energy, or intensity of which one is capable [14]–receive! In other words <u>adoption is a process</u>. The adoption as children of God is a process of repenting, yielding, learning, a process of being trained and disciplined by the Holy Spirit. Notice it says we have the privilege of becoming. We have the power to become. Under the tutorage of the Holy Spirit we are trained as sons. The Holy Spirit trains us just as The Word says in Proverbs *"Train up a child in the way he should go, and when he is old he* **<u>will not depart</u>** *from it."* [15] Paul, again speaking to the Hebrews says, *"But solid food is for the mature, who because of practice have their senses* **<u>trained</u>** *to discern good and evil."* [16] *"All discipline for the moment seems not to be joyful, but sorrowful; yet to those* **who have been trained by it,** *afterwards it yields the peaceful fruit of righteousness."* [17] So we see here that we need to be trained to 'become' or *undergo the change and development* that will bring about the transformation into sons of God. *"Blessed are the peacemakers: for they shall be called the children of God."* [18] *"Having <u>predestinated us unto the adoption</u> of children by Jesus Christ to Himself, according to the good pleasure of His will."* [19] *"For ye are all the children of God <u>by faith</u> in Christ Jesus. For as many of you <u>as have been baptized into Christ have put on Christ</u>."* [20] *"For it became Him, for whom are all things, and by whom are all things, in bringing many sons unto glory, to make the captain of their salvation perfect through sufferings...."* [21] Let me say here that you don't work for your Salvation, you surrender to the Holy Spirit in Christ by **faith** and are saved. It's not working as in doing things that make you right. You are right by justification; because you trusted the work of Christ on the cross. You trusted that what He did in His death was enough, but by your yielding to the Spirit of Christ within you, you begin to walk uprightly. Predestined means 'determined before hand;' it does not mean that there are certain individuals God has chosen before birth who will with no volition of their own become children of God. It does mean He determined beforehand that all who receive Him, those who under conviction of the Holy Spirit, yield and surrender, will become children of God; those who through faith, i.e. trusting and relying on, who <u>continue to undergo change and development into the transformation</u> He intended beforehand. As you seek Him, your heart and mind's desire will be to do those things that are pleasing to Him. He will not guide you into error. It becomes your joy to walk in obedience. You respond out of love for Him, not duty. When you were a child, did you not do things that pleased your earthly father and mother because it brought them joy? You received joy because you gave joy. It's the same in our relationship with God, Jesus and the Holy Spirit; as you walk in obedience you give them joy and in return you have joy. It is not drudgery to walk after the righteous ways of God; it is JOY! *"fixing our eyes on Jesus, the author and **perfecter** of our faith, **who for the joy set before Him endured the cross**, despising the shame, and has sat down at the right hand of the throne of God."* [22] *"Therefore, if there is any encouragement in Christ, If there is any consolation of love, if there is any fellowship of the Spirit, if any affection and compassion, make my joy complete by being of the same mind maintaining the same love, united in spirit, intent on one purpose. Do nothing from selfishness or empty conceit, but with humility of mind regard one another as more important than yourselves; do not merely look out for your own personal interest, but also for the interest of others. Have this attitude in yourselves which was also in Christ Jesus.......* [23]*'**the joy that was set before Him**!'* So it is with us; our joy is a result of obedience because we know it brings Him joy.

"*Blessed be the God and Father of our Lord Jesus Christ, who according to His great mercy has caused us to be born again to a living hope through the resurrection of Jesus Christ from the dead, to obtain an inheritance which is imperishable and undefiled and will not fade away, reserved in heaven for you, who are **protected by the power of God through faith** for a salvation ready to be revealed in the last time. In this you **greatly rejoice**, even though now for a little while, if necessary, you have been distressed by various trials, so **that the proof of your faith**, being more precious than gold which is perishable, even though tested by fire, may be found to **result in praise and glory and honor** at the revelation of Jesus Christ; and though you have not seen Him, you love Him, and though you do not see Him now, but believe in Him, **you greatly rejoice with joy** inexpressible and full of glory…*"[24] So in Salvation you leave the old nature of sin, your old father the devil and enter into the privileges and responsibilities of God, through Jesus Christ. Remember in Genesis when God said, "Therefore a man shall *leave* his father and mother…." Did you take that to mean he'll put them off for a little while yet they will sometimes get the best of him? Wavering as to whether he wanted to be with his parents or with his wife? No; you understood it to mean he would leave their household and begin a new household with his wife, never to return again to live with them. The connotation is the same with Salvation you leave-*as in never to return to your old life style*, i.e. nature. You put it off, do away with it, and leave it. In Romans 7:24 Paul says, *"O wretched man that I am! Who will deliver me from this body of death?"* This is a picture of 'a person chained to a corpse from which he cannot be freed, despairing of deliverance.' Then Paul goes on to say in verse 25 *"I thank God —-through Jesus Christ our Lord!"* The victory is in Jesus; He is able to deliver us from this body of death; this body of death he is speaking of is sin! Jesus, through His death, burial and resurrection has delivered us from sin! When you are delivered from something it no longer has control over you. You are free. If you are freed from being chained to a corpse, would you go back to being chained to one again to that corpse? That is how we should view sin, as repulsive as a dead corpse.

WHAT IS ADOPTION?

In Baker's Evangelical Dictionary of Biblical Theology, it is stated that adoption is an "Act of *leaving one's natural family and entering into the privileges and responsibilities of another*." The English Standard Version of the text in Ephesians 1:5 states, *"He predestined us for adoption through Jesus Christ, according to the purpose of His will."* there is a notation stating:

> "Adoption" (Greek *huiothesia*, meaning *placing as a son* is not so much a word of relationship as it is of position. In regeneration, a Christian receives the nature of a child of God; in adoption he receives the position of a son of God. Every Christian obtains the place of a child and the right to be called a son the moment he believes (Galatians 3:25; 4:6; 1 John 3:1, 2) The indwelling Spirit gives the realization of this in the Christian's present experience (Galatians 4:6); but the full manifestation of his sonship awaits the resurrection, change, and translation of saints, which is called the "redemption of our bodies."(Romans 8:23; Ephesians 1:14; 1 Thessalonians. 4:14-17; 1 John 3:2).

Many years ago, while studying Romans, I found in a commentary (I do not recall which one at this time) an explanation given of the process of adoption in ancient Rome, where the son of the Roman father was trained up to be a 'son'. Upon fully training the son to carry out his affairs in his absence exactly as he would, the father would take the son to the court of law and legally adopt him as his 'son', i.e. heir of all. The son could then control all that belonged to the father. This is a picture of the Scripture in Galatians 4:1-2: *'Now I say, as long as the heir is a child, he does not differ at all from a slave although he is owner of everything, but he is under guardians and managers <u>until the date set by the father</u>.'* We too are under '*guardians and managers*' and being discipled by The Holy Spirit, pastors, teachers, elders and deacons set by God until the date set by our Father in heaven. It is when we <u>come under the authority</u> of those set over us by the Holy Spirit that we can be fully trained and ready for the adoption of a 'son'. If you will continue to study this portion of Scripture in Galatians, it says in verse five *"that we <u>might</u> receive the adoptions as sons"* and in verse nineteen Paul says, *"My children, whom I am again in labor <u>until</u> Christ is formed in you—"* in other words, Paul is saying you are not there yet, and he is desperately trying to get them to the place where they are ready to receive the adoption as sons. It is a process we are in, 'until Christ is formed in us'. When Christ is fully formed in us we will receive the adoption as sons. Galatians 5:5 states it this way: *"For we through the Spirit, by faith, are waiting for the hope of righteousness."*

SALVATION, IS IT FREE?

Let's consider the following saying: 'free gift of Salvation,' Salvation cost God His only Son! It was a very high price. Jesus Christ died a very cruel death and shed His blood to **pay the price** for our Salvation. You say, "Well it doesn't cost me anything!" It doesn't? Jesus, talking to the multitude about following Him, said that *"If anyone comes to Me and does not hate his own father and mother and wife and children and brothers and sisters, yes, even his own life, he cannot be My disciple. Whoever does not carry his own cross and come after Me cannot be My disciple. For which one of you, when he wants to build a tower, does not first sit down and <u>**calculate the cost**</u> to see if he has enough to complete it? Otherwise, when he has laid a foundation and is not able to finish, all who observe it begin to ridicule him, saying, 'This man began to build and was not able to finish' Or what king, when he sets out to meet another king in battle, **will not first <u>sit down and consider</u>** whether he is strong enough with ten thousand men to encounter the one coming against him with twenty thousand ² Or else, while the other is still far away, he sends a delegation and asks for terms of peace. So then, none of you can be My disciple who does not give up all his own possessions."* [25] This is a parable Jesus used to explain that very thing, the cost of your Salvation! So now tell me it cost you nothing! Hebrews 6:1-3 talks about the elementary principles

Salvation, Redemption

of Christ, which are the foundations of the gospel. I'll just name them here then make my point. 1. Repentance from dead works. 2. Faith toward God. 3. Doctrine of baptisms. 4. Laying on of hands. 5. Resurrection of the dead. 6. Eternal judgment. Continuing in that same chapter he talks about those who have been enlightened concerning the above six things, *"**if they fall away, it is impossible to renew them again unto repentance;** seeing they crucify to themselves the Son of God afresh, and put Him to an open shame."*[26] You tell me that is not costly! John 15 says those who do not produce fruit for the kingdom are fit for nothing but to be cut off the vine and burned. Notice they were a part of the vine, attached to the vine, yet they failed to produce fruit. What kind of fruit is Jesus referring to, Galatians tells us: *"But the fruit of the Spirit is love, joy, peace, longsuffering, gentleness, goodness, faith, meekness, temperance: against such there is no law."* [27] As a born again believer the Spirit will produce the fruit in us <u>as we are yielded;</u> body, soul and spirit, to Him and as we <u>abide</u> in the vine. Jesus said, "Y*e shall know them by their fruit. Do men gather grapes of thorns, or figs of thistles?"* [28] In this He was speaking of fruit in keeping with repentance as mentioned in an earlier chapter. In essence, what He is saying is that if you are 'saved' you will have evidence by the 'fruit' or actions of your life. If you are abiding in the Vine, God, Jesus, and the Holy Spirit in you will produce righteousness. 1 John 5:1-3a says, "W*hosoever believeth that Jesus is the Christ is born of God: and every one that loveth Him that begat loveth Him also that is begotten of Him. By this we know that we love the children of God, when we love God, and keep His commandments.* ***<u>For this is the love of God, that we keep His commandments</u>***..." And Paul says in Corinthians; *'For we are a fragrance of Christ to God among those who are **'being saved'** and among those who are perishing.'* [29] *"And ye shall be hated of all men for My name's sake:* ***<u>but he that endureth to the end shall be saved</u>****."* [30] *"And because iniquity shall abound, the love of many shall wax cold. But **<u>he that shall endure unto the end, the same shall be saved</u>**."* [31] ***Endure*** comes from the Greek word *hupomeno* which means: To hold one's ground in conflict, to bear up against adversity, hold out under stress, stand firm, persevere under pressure, wait calmly and courageously.[32]

I know this is a strong word BUT that **IS** the ***<u>Power</u> of Salvation*** to those who ***believe, i.e. trust***. Jesus death was not a cheap grace. The mercy and grace of God cost Jesus His life. Oh, what a precious life He gave. Don't take it for granted. Hebrews 2:3 says, *"how shall we escape if we **<u>neglect</u>** such a great salvation?"*

Christianity

HOW CAN WE KNOW WE ARE BEING SAVED?

MEDITATE on the following verses: *"This then message we have heard of Him and declare unto you, that God is light, and in Him is no darkness at all."* in God there is no darkness, evil or sin at all.

"If we say that we have fellowship with Him, and walk in darkness, we lie, and do not the truth:"... If we walk (implies a habitual mode of living) in sin, keep sinning and can't help it, we cannot have fellowship with God. *"If we say that we have no sin, we deceive ourselves,"*.... If we say that we have not sinned, that all our actions are right, that we do no wrong. Or *"If we say that we have not sinned, we make Him a liar, and His word is not in us."* By thinking that 'I'm a good person' or excusing our sin by judging or comparing ours lives with the actions of others, we make God a liar. But when (as an exception) we commit an act of sin i.e., miss the mark or stumble, *"IF we confess our sins,"* (as in confessing the actual sin) He is faithful and just to forgive us our sin and cleanse us from all unrighteousness. [33] *"My little children, these things write I unto you, **THAT YE SIN NOT**. And if any man sin, we have an Advocate with the Father, Jesus Christ the righteous:"* [34] In other words, you won't continue to habitually sin with no will of your own (I can't help it). You may stumble on occasion but it will not be a continual, habitual mode of living. Many sincere people pray for forgiveness of sin every time they pray; I'm not saying it is wrong, because they may have 'missed the mark' unknowingly. When a Christian sins, the Holy Spirit convicts them almost immediately and at that moment they are to confess that sin. 1 John 5:14-15 says, *"And this is the confidence that we have in Him, that, if we ask any thing according to His will, He heareth us; and if we know that He hears us, whatsoever we ask, we know that we have the petitions that we desired of Him."* So, when we sin and are convicted by the Holy Spirit and confess that sin, IT IS FORGIVEN, period! We need not continually ask forgiveness for that sin. If we are questioning whether or not we are forgiven, we do not have confidence and therefore do not have faith. James tells us to *"ask without doubt because if we doubt we know we will not get anything from the Lord."* [35] Doubt reveals a divided heart toward God and His word. Read all of 1 JOHN 3:1-24, here I will quote a portion of it:

"By this the children of God and the children of the devil are obvious: **anyone who does not practice righteousness is not of God**, *nor the one who does not love his brother. .... We know that we have passed out of death into life, **because we love the brethren**. **He who does not love abides in death**... .... This is His commandment that we believe in the name of His Son Jesus Christ, and love one another, just as He commanded us.* **The**

*one who keeps **His commandments abides in Him**, and He in him. We know by this that He abides in us, by the Spirit whom He has given us."* [36] We see here that those who practice righteousness love the brethren and those who keep God's commandments abide in Him; these are those who are being saved.

TEST THE SPIRITS: This is how you will know whether you are walking after the Spirit of Christ or the spirit of the devil; *"Do not be <u>bound together</u> with unbelievers; for what <u>partnership</u> have righteousness and lawlessness, or what <u>fellowship</u> has light with darkness? Or what <u>harmony</u> has Christ with Belial (Satan), or what has a believer in common with an unbeliever? Or what <u>agreement</u> has the temple of God with idols? For we are the temple of the living God; just as God said, "I WILL DWELL IN THEM AND WALK AMONG THEM; AND I WILL BE THEIR GOD, AND THEY SHALL BE MY PEOPLE. "Therefore, COME OUT FROM THEIR MIDST AND <u>**BE SEPEARATE**</u>," says the Lord. "AND **<u>DO NOT TOUCH</u>** <u>WHAT IS UNCLEAN</u>; And I will welcome you. "And I will be a father to you, and you shall be sons and daughters to Me," Says the Lord Almighty.* 7:1 *"Therefore, having these promises, beloved,* **let us cleanse ourselves from all defilement of flesh and spirit, perfecting holiness in the fear of God."* [37] Note the first six words I underlined in the previous Scripture: *bound together, partnership, fellowship, harmony* and *agreement*. All of these words symbolize relationship; close relationship. Harmony and agreement symbolize *no division but unity*. In Amos 3:3 it says, *"Can two walk together unless they be agreed?"* By implication, how can you get along with someone you don't agree with? You can't! Remember in repentance <u>you have had a change of mind and change of heart</u> toward sin. You no longer agree that it's ok. It is abhorrence to a Holy God! So here we see that those who separate themselves from the world, i.e. the world's philosophies, fads, rhetoric, life styles, etc., those who don't <u>fellowship</u> with those of the world, are being saved. Let's look at another portion of Scripture: *"Therefore, prepare your minds for action, keep sober in spirit, <u>fix</u> your hope completely on the grace to be brought to you at the revelation of Jesus Christ. As obedient children,* **do not be conformed to the former lusts** *which were yours in your ignorance, but like the Holy One who called you,* **be holy yourselves also in all your behavior**; *because it is written,* **"YOU SHALL BE HOLY, FOR I AM HOLY."** *If you address as Father the One ......,* **conduct yourselves in fear** <u>during the time of your stay on earth</u>; *knowing that you were not redeemed with perishable things like silver or gold <u>from your futile way of life</u> inherited from your forefathers, but with precious blood, as of a* *lamb unblemished and spotless, the blood of Christ......so that your faith and hope are in God.* **Since you have in <u>obedience to the truth purified your souls</u> for a sincere love of the brethren, fervently love one another from the heart, for you have been born again not of seed which is perishable but imperishable**, *that is, through the living and enduring word of God."* [38] Those that <u>practice</u> holiness; purifying their souls, rather than continuing in or falling back into the former lifestyle are being saved. Remember your soul is your intellect or mind, your <u>will</u> and your emotions. You purify something by a washing/cleaning agent. You purify your souls by the *"washing of the water by the Word."* [39] As you study the Word of God it washes out the dead corrupt thoughts and ideas and puts in new, life giving thoughts and ideas, or as Romans 12:2 says you are: *"transformed you by the renewing of your mind."* Your intellect is purified-you no longer meditate, seek, read, allow to come into your mind things of evil, [40] your will (volition) or your 'want to' is purified. You do not want to sin. You do not want to read, watch or hear anything that would disgust a Holy God or grieve the Holy Spirit. You now abhor sin as God does. And lastly your emotions: the heart is the seat of the emotions, so your heart does not want to act in a way that disgraces the Spirit of Truth. *"Therefore, putting aside all malice and all deceit and hypocrisy and envy and all slander, like newborn babies,* **long for the pure milk of the word**, *so that by it* **<u>you may grow in respect to salvation</u>**, *if you have tasted the kindness of the Lord."* [41] Those who desire the Word of God, who are growing in respect to salvation, are being saved. Remember the word salvation means delivered, rescued, victory, aid, health, and safe or safety, prosperity, liberation, being made whole, body, soul and spirit. *"So this I say and solemnly testify in [the name of] the Lord [as in His presence], that* **<u>you must no longer live</u>** *as the heathen (the Gentiles) do in their perverseness [in the folly, vanity, and emptiness of their souls and the futility] of their minds. Their moral understanding is darkened and their reasoning is beclouded. [They are] alienated (**<u>estranged</u>**, **<u>self-banished</u>**) from the life of God [with no share in it; this is] because of the ignorance (the want of knowledge and perception, the* **willful blindness***) that is deep-seated in them,* **<u>due to their hardness of heart</u>** *[to the insensitiveness of their moral nature]. In their spiritual apathy they have become callous and past feeling and reckless and have abandoned themselves [a prey] to unbridled sensuality, eager and greedy to indulge in every form of impurity [that their depraved desires may suggest and demand]. But you did not so learn Christ!* [42] *"***IF THEN** *you have been raised with Christ [to a new life, thus sharing His resurrection from the dead], aim at and seek the [rich, eternal treasures]* *that are above, where Christ is, seated at the right hand of God. And set your minds and keep them set on what is above (the higher things), not on the things that are on the earth. For [as far as this world is concerned] you have died, and your [new, real] life is hidden with Christ in God."* [43] *"Beloved, I implore you as aliens and strangers and exiles [in this world] to abstain from the sensual urges (the evil desires, the passions of the flesh, your lower nature) that wage war against the soul."* [44] *"FOR BY GRACE ARE YE SAVED through faith; and that not of yourselves: it is the gift of God: not of works, lest any man should boast."* [45] Oh, IT IS a gift of God! But, it is a gift that is not free. Remember the cost to Him. You can't do anything in and of yourself to obtain Salvation that is why it is a gift. He offers it to you but you are accountable for what you do with the gift He offers to you. You don't take it and set it on a shelf and wait 'till' you die to receive His promises of Salvation, it's for here and now. Hebrews 2:3 says, **"how shall we escape if we ignore such a great salvation?"** You don't put down a foundation for a house and never build the walls and roof, or you would not have a house. You build upon it! Remember earlier I referred to Hebrews 6, concerning the FOUNDATION of the Gospel. Paul says, *"By the grace God has given me, I laid a foundation as an expert builder, and someone else is building on it.* **But each one should be careful how he builds.** *For no one can lay any foundation other than the one already laid, which is Jesus Christ."* [46]

Testing the spirits involves checking our attitudes and actions and the attitudes and actions of those we fellowship with by the Word of God. Repentance will change our heart and mind about our lifestyle. If nothing has changed, we need to check our relationship with the Father. What are you doing with the gift of Salvation?

How Our Confession and Belief as Christians Effects our Salvation

'But what saith it? The word is nigh thee, even in thy mouth, and in thy heart: that is, the word of faith, which we preach; That if thou shalt confess with thy mouth the Lord Jesus, and shalt believe in thine heart that God hath raised him from the dead, thou shalt be saved. For with the heart man believeth unto righteousness; and with the mouth confession is made unto salvation." [47] *This is the message we have heard from Him and announce to you; that God is Light, and in Him there is no darkness at all. If we say that we have fellowship with Him yet walk in the darkness, we lie and do not practice the truth;* **but if we walk in the Light, as He is in the Light, we have fellowship with one another, and the blood of Jesus His Son, cleanses us from ALL SIN.** *If we say we have no sin, we*

are deceiving ourselves and the truth is not in us." [48] Heart belief results in righteous living because you choose to walk in the light of the Word. This is not from yourself but from the power of the Holy Spirit that has been invested in you through your new birth. We are to walk in the Light as He is in the Light. We are to imitate Christ. We are to walk like our Daddy (God the Father). We are no longer children of the devil. We are to daily to obey our Spiritual Daddy (God the Father) with the help of the Holy Spirit within us. Because we <u>were</u> (past tense) redeemed (bought by the blood of Jesus) we now have the <u>power walk</u>- not to sin. Jesus said, *"However, I am telling you nothing but the truth when I say it is profitable (good, expedient, advantageous) for you that I go away. Because if I do not go away, the Comforter (Counselor, Helper, Advocate, Intercessor, Strengthener, Standby) will not come to you [into close fellowship with you]; but if I go away, I will send Him to you [to be in close fellowship with you]."* [49] Our belief must line up with our confession. If we say one thing and do the opposite, God says we are a liar. Our actions must line up with our confession.

Chapter Eight

[1] # 3444 *y shuw 'ah'* [6]
[2] # 4991 *soterion* [6]
[3] John 3:16
[4] John 1: 9-13
[5] John 3:3
[6] John 3: 6
[7] John 3:5
[8] John 3:16-18
[9] #1350 *ga'al* & 6299 *padah* [6]
[10] #629 & 630 *apoluo*, 3085 *lutrosis* [6]
[11] John 1:12
[12] Romans 8:14-15
[13] Galatians 4:4-5
[14] Page 537 [7]
[15] Proverbs 22:6
[16] Hebrews 5:14 [4]
[17] Hebrews 12:11 [4]
[18] Matthew 5:9
[19] Ephesians 1:5
[20] Galatians 3:26-27
[21] Hebrews 2:10-11
[22] Hebrews 12:2 [4]
[23] Philippians 2:1-5a [4]
[24] 1Peter 1:3-8 [4]
[25] Luke 14: 26-33 [4]
[26] Hebrews 6:6 [8]
[27] Galatians 5:22-23
[28] Matthew 7:16
[29] 2 Corinthians 2:15 [8]
[30] Matthew 10:22
[31] Matthew 24:12-13
[32] Page 5278 [6]
[33] 1 John 1:1-8
[34] 1 John 2:1
[35] James 1:7
[36] I John 3:10, 14, 23-24 [8]
[37] 2 Corinthians 6:16-7:1 [4]

[38] 1 Peter 1:13-23
[39] Ephesians 5:26
[40] 1Thessalonians 5:22 'abstain from every form of evil'
[41] 1 Peter 2:1-3 [4]
[42] Ephesians 4:17-20 [1]
[43] Colossians 3:1-3 [1]
[44] 1 Peter 2:11 [1]
[45] Ephesians 2:8-9
[46] 1 Corinthians 3:10-11 [5]
[47] Romans 10:8-10
[48] 1 John 1:5-8 [4]
[49] John 16:7 [1]

Chapter Nine

Salvation is Through None Other Than Jesus Christ

who said, "I am <u>The</u> Way, <u>The</u> Truth and <u>The</u> Life." [1]

N otice "I am *THE*"; 'The' is a definite article meaning there is no other, I'm it! We will discuss the Fathers' role, Jesus' role, Holy Spirit's role and our role in Salvation. But for now let's look at the first step in salvation. John the Baptist said, **"Repent for the Kingdom of Heaven is at hand."**[2] And Jesus said, **"Repent for the Kingdom of Heaven is at hand."** [3] Peter said, **"Repent, and be baptized every one of you in the name of Jesus Christ for the remission of sins; and ye shall receive the gift of the Holy Ghost."** [4]

The one word that resounded in what John the Baptist, Jesus and Peter said was **"Repent"!** You see, where there is no *repentance* there can be no Salvation, *"The Lord is not slack concerning His promise, as some men count slackness; but is longsuffering to us-ward, not willing that any to perish, but that **all to come to repentance.**"* [5] The very meaning of repentance brings about a change. What is repentance? Remember earlier when I spoke of the flood, and how God repented that He had made man? In parenthesis I put He had <u>a change of mind and heart; He was sorry and grieved in His heart</u>. In repentance you have a change of mind and heart. What do you 'repent' of? To answer that-ask yourself, 'what are you saved from'? Many people I've ask what are you saved from replied, "From hell." That is true but not in the truest sense of Salvation. Some reply, "SIN." But if you ask them if they still sin they will say, "Sure, we all do. No one can live in this world and not sin." If you are SAVED from something it no longer has control over you. The Bible says in, John 1:29 *"Behold, the Lamb of God, **which taketh away the sin of the world!**"* Jesus came to save you from sin! What caused Adam and Eve to fall ....it was sin. Does this sound confusing to you? How can someone take something from me and I still possess it? Let's look at the phrase 'take away the sin of the world,' if I take something away from you do you still have it? No! I've got it! It is no longer with you, right? Well, when the Word of God says that Jesus (the Lamb) *taketh away* the sin of the world, what does that mean? 'Taketh' in the Greek means to bear away, remove, put away, to lift up or away.[6] Note also the 'eth' which means a continual process.

WHAT'S GOD THE FATHERS' PART IN OUR SALVATION?

*"For God so loved the world, that **HE GAVE** His only begotten Son, that whoever **believeth** in Him should not perish, but have everlasting life. "For God sent not His Son into the world to condemn the world; but that the world through Him might be saved."* [7] *"Yet **it was the LORD'S will to crush** Him and **cause Him to suffer**, and though **the LORD makes His life a guilt offering**, He will see His offspring and prolong His days, and the will of the LORD will prosper in His hand."* [8] *We all, like sheep, have gone astray, each of us has turned to his own way; and the LORD has **laid on Him the iniquity of us all**.* [9] Paul says in Corinthians that *"For **He made Him** who knew no sin **to be sin for us**, that we might become the righteousness of God in Him."* [10] Isaiah's prophecy concerning Jesus in chapter 53:1-12 states that there was nothing to attract us to Him, He wasn't handsome or regal, His appearance did nothing to draw us to Him; He was an outcast, suffered much and yet He took our diseases and frailties upon Himself. Yet we *'considered **Him stricken by God, smitten by Him, and afflicted. But He was pierced for our transgressions, He was crushed for our iniquities;**'* and the price for our sin He willingly paid, He received the punishment so we could have peace and He took a beating so that we might be healed. But we have done our own thing and gone our own way yet *'**the LORD has laid on Him the iniquity of us all.**'* Though He went through all this He did not defend Himself, but went willingly like *'a lamb to the slaughter and as a sheep before her shearers is silent*, He spoke not a word. ***By oppression and judgment He was taken away.*** He had no children of His own, *'For **He was cut off from the land of the living; for the transgression of My people He was stricken**. He was assigned a grave with the wicked and with the rich in His death, though He had done no violence, nor was any deceit in His mouth. Yet it was the*

<u>**LORD'S will to crush Him and cause Him to suffer**</u>, *and though* <u>**the LORD makes His life a guilt offering**</u>, *He will see His offspring and prolong His days, and the will of the LORD will prosper in His hand."* Jesus said in John;*" No one can come to Me unless* **the Father** *who sent Me draws him:"* [11]

The Father's part: the Father *gave Him*, He was *stricken, smitten and afflicted* by the Father, the Father *crushed Him*, the Father *cut Him off from the land of the living*, the Father *caused Him to suffer*, and the Father *made His life a guilt offering*. It is the Father who *draws us* to Himself.

WHAT WAS/IS JESUS' PART?

Look back up at the previously quoted scripture from Isaiah. *He took up our infirmities and carried our sorrows, He was pierced for our transgressions, He was crushed for our iniquities; the punishment that brought us peace was upon Him, and by His wounds we are healed. He poured out his life unto death, was numbered with the transgressors. He bore the sin of many and made intercession for the transgressors.* [12] Jesus confession in Luke, before His crucifixion: *"It is written: 'And He was numbered with the transgressors'; and I tell you that* <u>***this must be fulfilled in Me***</u>*. Yes, what is written about Me is reaching its fulfillment."* [13] *"For if while we were enemies we were reconciled to God through the* **death of His Son**, *much more, having been reconciled,* **we shall be saved by His life**.*"* [14] *"but the gift of God is eternal life* **in Christ Jesus our Lord**.*"* [15] *"He came to His own, and those who were His own did not receive Him." "But as many as* **received Him**, *to them* <u>**He gave the right to become children of God**</u>, *even to those who* **believe** *in His name,"* [16]

Jesus' part: He fulfilled what the Father sent Him to do in every way. He did not lack even unto death in fulfilling the Father's will. As mentioned earlier, He destroyed the Devil and his power in the earth, disarming him and causing a spectacle of him.

WHAT IS THE HOLY SPIRIT'S PART?

The Holy Spirit overshadowed i.e., brooded (just as in creation) over Mary and Jesus was conceived in her womb. *The angel answered,* **"The Holy Spirit will come upon you, and the power of the Most High will overshadow you.** *So the holy one to be born will be called the Son of God"* [17] Simeon, a devout follower of God, had been promised that he would not die until he had seen the promised Messiah. When the time came for Jesus mother and Joseph to bring Jesus to the temple for His circumcision the Holy Spirit sent Simeon to the temple at the same time and upon seeing

Jesus took Him in his arms and blessed God then said to God that he could now depart in peace because he had seen The Salvation of Israel. [18]

The Holy Spirits' part: Jesus was conceived by the Holy Spirit, The Holy Spirit revealed God and His plan to certain individuals, The Holy Spirit moves people to do things, i.e. to write the Biblical record. Speaking of the Holy Spirit Jesus said, *"And when He has come, He will **convict the world of sin**, and of righteousness and of judgment:"* [18] so the Holy Spirit **convicts of sin.** In Luke 12:12 and 1 Corinthians 2:13 **He is our teacher,** in Ephesians 1:13 **He seals us,** in 1 Peter 1:12 He **enables us to preach the Gospel**. More will be said of the Holy Spirits role in our lives in another chapter.

WHAT IS OUR PART?

Repent, Believe (trust), and Receive, Walk and Rest!

Repent was the command of John the Baptist, Peter and Jesus. *In those days John the Baptist came, preaching in the Desert of Judea and saying, "**Repent**, for the kingdom of heaven is near."* [19] *"And so John came....... preaching a **baptism of repentance** for the forgiveness of sins."* [20] *"Jesus began to preach, "**Repent**, ."* [21] *"I have not come to call the righteous, but sinners to **repentance**."* [22] *"They went out and preached that **people should repent**."* [23] *"I have declared ... that **they must turn to God in repentance and have faith in our Lord Jesus**.* [24] *"In the past God overlooked such ignorance, but now He commands **all people everywhere to repent**."* [25]

Believe- *"that everyone who **believes** in Him may have eternal life. For God so loved the world ..., that **whoever believes in Him shall not perish** but have eternal life."* [26] *"**Believe in the Lord Jesus, and you will be saved**—."* [27] *..... but **by faith** in Jesus Christ. ... put our faith (**believe**) in Christ Jesus that we may be justified by faith in Christ ....* [28] *and be found in Him, ... **through faith** in Christ—the righteousness that comes from God and is by **faith**:* [29] *"For it is by grace you have been saved, **through faith**—and this not from yourselves, it is the gift of God"* [30] *We live **by faith**, not by sight.* [31] *Whoever **believes** in Him is not condemned, but whoever does not believe stands condemned already because he has not believed in the name of God's one and only Son.* [32] *Whoever **believes in the Son has eternal life**,"* [33] *"I tell you the truth, whoever hears My word and **believes** Him who sent Me has eternal life ...has crossed over from death to life."* [34] Through faith *in*, believes *in* Him, faith *in* Christ Jesus, found *in* Him; remember in Chapter three I said the word '*in*' is a function word that meant *the same nature of*; here we see that believing causes us to have the same nature of Christ, i.e. the restored likeness and image of God. The Old Testament word in Genesis 15:6 for 'believe' meant not only to trust, but to be faithful for a long continuance, to be steadfast or resolute, to be established, and to turn to the right. In other words, Abram trusted God to establish His word to him without reservation. He placed his life in God's control. **Believe** in Greek is *pist-yoo'o-* to have faith (in, upon, or with respect to a person or thing, to entrust, commit (from the word *pis'-tis* which means persuasion, credence; moral conviction, especially reliance upon Christ for salvation) "***Believe*** according to Strong's Concordance is the verb form of faith. It means **to trust in, have faith in, be fully convinced of, acknowledge, and** *rely on*. Believe is not just adhering to 'church' doctrine nor is it belonging to a certain church. It is about trust in and reliance upon the One who has the power to deliver. It brings us to the place of willing obedience, not only recognizing but submitting to the Lordship of Jesus Christ.

Receive "*To this John replied, "A man can receive only what is given him from heaven.*"[35] *Whoever in My name and for My sake accepts **and receives** and welcomes one such child also accepts **and receives** and welcomes Me; and whoever so **receives Me** receives not only Me but Him Who sent Me.*" [36] "*But as many as received Him, to them He gave the right to become children of God,*" [37]"*Therefore as you have **received** Christ Jesus the Lord, so walk in Him,*" [38] "*Therefore, since we **receive a kingdom** which cannot be shaken, let us show gratitude, by which we may offer to God an acceptable service with reverence and awe;*" [39]

Let's look at the word *received* and a word many use when referring to receiving Christ as Savior: *accept*. I've heard many people say that if you *accept* Jesus Christ as your Savior, you will be saved. I have not seen the word *accept* alone in reference to salvation in Scripture. Of all the above Scriptures mention the word says *received* Him. The word received has a totally different meaning than the word accept.

> ***Accept*** according to Webster's means *to receive with consent, to give admittance or approval too, to regard as proper, normal or inevitable, and to receive into the mind.* In other words you come to believe something is true or

regard it as true or inevitable. It does <u>not</u> however mean you actually depend upon it.

Now *receive* according to Webster's *means to* **take or come into the possession of***, to take in: hold,* **contain***, to take in through the mind or senses,* **to permit to enter***, admit, welcome, greet,* **to undergo experience***.*

You can see that receive means much more than accepting something as true. You have an experience where you take possession of something; you hold it within and contain it into your being. Salvation is believing—which is receiving, not just accepting. Can you see the difference? What the Word or Scripture says about believing is therefore receiving Christ as your Savior: *"So that whoever **believes** will in Him have eternal life."* [40] Now in the following chapter we will discuss how the believing i.e. receiving becomes our born again experience or birthright.

Rest- God had prepared a place of rest and safety for Israel in the land of Canaan where He had led them out of Egypt. However, because of unbelief and disobedience they wondered in the wilderness for forty years. In Hebrews 2:10-14, God says He was grieved with Israel because they kept 'erring' in their heart. What they actually did was not trust Him, and the result was that He wouldn't let them enter into His rest. The writer of Hebrews warns us to; *"Take heed, brethren, lest <u>there be in any of you an evil heart of unbelief,</u> in departing from the living God. But exhort one another daily, while it is called today; lest any of you be <u>hardened through the deceitfulness of sin</u>. For we are made partakers of Christ, <u>IF</u> we hold fast the beginning of our confidence to the end."* Verse nineteen of this chapter says, *"So we see that they could not enter in because of unbelief."* Then verse one of chapter four says, *'Let us therefore fear, lest, a promise being left us of entering into his rest, <u>any of you should seem to come short of it</u>."* We enter the rest of God by trusting in, relying on, and adhering to the substitutionary death, burial and resurrection of Jesus Christ. *"Almost all things are by the law purged with blood; and without the shedding of blood; there is no remission of sin."*[41] We do not work for our Salvation; we work it out by the renewing of our minds. [42] Christ did the work; we rest by faith i.e., trust in what He did at Calvary.

CHAPTER NINE

[1] John 14:6
[2] Matthew 3:2
[3] Matthew 4:17
[4] Acts 2:38
[5] 2 Peter 3:9
[6] #142[6]
[7] John 3:16-17
[8] Isaiah 53:10 [5]
[9] Isaiah 53:6 5
[10] 2 Corinthians 5:21[8]
[11] John 6:44
[12] Isaiah 53: 1-10
[13] Luke 22:37
[14] Romans 5:10
[15] Romans 6:23b
[16] John 1:11-12
[17] Luke 1:26-35
[18] Luke 2:25- 32
[18] John 16:8
[19] Matthew 3:1-2
[20] Mark 1:4
[21] Matthew 4:17
[22] Luke 5:32
[23] Mark 6:12
[24] Acts 20:21
[25] Acts 17:30
[26] John 3:15-16
[27] Acts 16:31
[28] Galatians 2:16
[29] Philippians 3:9
[30] Ephesians 2:8
[31] 2Co 5:7
[32] John 3:18
[33] John 3:36
[34] John 5:24
[35] John 3:27
[36] Mark 9:37[1]

[37] John 1:12
[38] Colossians 2:6
[39] Hebrews 12:28
[40] John 3:15
[41] Hebrews 9:22
[42] Philippians 2:12 & Romans 12: 2

Chapter Ten

Born Again – Our Birthright

How to Be Born Again

*"Flesh **gives birth** to flesh, but the Spirit **gives birth** to spirit. You should not be surprised at My saying, 'You **must** be **born again**,"* [1] *"He chose to **give us birth** through the Word of Truth, that we might be a kind of firstfruits of all He created."* [2] *"Verily, verily, I say unto thee, except a man **be born again**, he cannot see the kingdom of God."* [3] *"He saved us, not because of righteous things we had done, but because of His mercy. He saved us through the washing of **rebirth** and renewal by the Holy Spirit."* [4]

To begin this discussion let me ask you some questions. What had to happen before Jesus could be resurrected? He had to submit to death! How did Abraham [5] conceive and bring forth the son of promise? Not until he, considering in spite of the *dead*ness of his own flesh, believed God. God waited until both Abraham and Sarah's ability to reproduce was impossible-they were both *dead* in the natural physical ability to produce children. Only God could produce the birth of Isaac. So how are we born again? <u>**We must die**</u>! We'll look at some of the Parables of Jesus to show us. Why look at parables? Jesus told disciples the purpose of the Parables. He answered and said to them, *"Because it has been given unto you <u>to know the mysteries of the kingdom</u> of heaven, but to <u>them</u> it is not given."* [6] Who is the '<u>them</u>?' It is unbelievers. In this particular instance it was the multitudes-look at verse two of the same chapter. (Keep in mind that we are taking all Scripture within the context of the chapter it is taken from as well as the audience being spoken to.)

Now the parables:

In John, just before Jesus was to be crucified after His triumphant entry into Jerusalem, there were some Greeks who were wanting to see Jesus, when Philip and Andrew, His disciples came and told Jesus. *He replied, "The hour has come that the Son of Man should be glorified. Most assuredly, I say to you, unless a grain of wheat falls into the ground <u>and dies,</u> it remains alone; but <u>if it dies</u>, it produces much grain. He who loves his life will lose it (die), and he who hates his life in this world will keep it for eternal life. If anyone **serves Me**, let him **follow Me**; and where I am, there My servant will be also. If anyone serves Me, him My Father will honor."*[7] Why was he talking about grain dying and where was He going? How were they to follow Him? Jesus was preparing to go to the Cross. What for? To die! Why? That He might return to the Father and be glorified! We know that when a grain of seed dries up it remains dormant until it is buried and watered. Then and only then can it bring forth new life. What does that have to do with us? Just like Jesus, the disciples and we too are to die to self, looking to the cross and identify with His death, seeing ourselves upon that cross in Him. (Not physically but through the soul-i.e. mind, will and emotions), if we look to the cross of Jesus and identify with His death, recognizing that when He died He died once for all to sin (just as Adam died once for all to the glory of God). We, being in Him, will be resurrected to newness of life. In Matthew 16:25 Jesus said, *"For whoever wants to save his life will lose it, but whoever loses his life for Me will find it."* We don't die physically, just as Adam and Eve in the Garden of Eden didn't immediately die physically. But we die to the sin nature that became inherent in us in the Garden, just as Adam and Eve died to the glory of God in the Garden and received the nature of the Devil i.e., the sin nature. We go to the cross of Christ and die to the old sin nature! Paul says, *"May it never be! How shall we who <u>died to sin</u> still live in it? Or do you not know that <u>**all of us who have been baptized into Christ Jesus have been baptized into His death**</u>? Therefore **<u>we have been buried with Him through baptism into death</u>**, so that as Christ was raised from the dead through the glory of the Father, so we too might walk in newness of life. <u>**For if we have become united with Him in the likeness of His death**</u>, certainly we shall also be in the likeness of His resurrection, knowing this, that **<u>our old self was crucified</u>** with Him, in order **that <u>our body of sin might be done away with</u>,** so that we would **<u>no longer be slaves to sin</u>;** for **<u>he who has died IS FREED FROM SIN</u>**.*"[8] Notice the underlined statement: 'our body of sin might be done away with;' correlate that with Jesus 'taking away our sin'—it's gone!

Remember that Adam and Eve were created with the same nature of God in the beginning, but through disobedience-SIN-they died to the glory of God within them and took on the nature of Satan or the Devil, and became his children. [9] So now, for us to become the children of God, we have to die to the nature of Satan, [10] and be born of the Spirit of God to become His children and receive His Glory which Adam and Eve forfeited. *"Blessed be the God and Father of our Lord Jesus Christ, who according to His great mercy He has caused us to be born again to a living hope through the resurrection of Jesus Christ from the dead,"* [11] *"children born not of natural descent, nor of human decision or a husband's will, but **born of God**.* [12] *"For you have **been born again** not of seed which is perishable, but imperishable, that is, **through the living and enduring word of God**."* [13] *"If you know that He is righteous, you know that everyone who practices righteousness is born of Him."* [14] Let's look at the two Scriptures I referred to in John & Matthew. In John, Jesus is talking to the Jews. *"If you abide in My word, you are My disciples indeed. And you shall know the truth and the truth shall make you free."* They replied, *"We are Abraham's descendants and have never been in bondage to anyone."* (Whoa! At that very time they were under the control of the Roman government, and had as a nation been in bondage numerous times, Egyptian, Babylonian, etc.) *"How can you say, You will be made free?" Jesus answered them, "Most assuredly, I say to you **whoever commits sin is a slave of sin**. And a slave does not abide in the house forever, but a son abides forever. Therefore if the Son makes you free, you shall be free indeed."* [15] Then He tells them, *"You are of your father the devil, and you want to do the desires of your father.* [16] So they continue to desire the things of the flesh, they are still slaves of sin, so they belong to the devil!

Now let's look at Matthew. Jesus is explaining the Parable of the Wheat and Tares. *'He answered and said unto them: "He that soweth the good seed is the Son of Man;* (referring to Himself). *The field is the world* (people); *the good seed are the children of the kingdom* (Christians); *but the tares are the children of the wicked one* (unbelievers). *The enemy that sowed them is the devil."* [17] We see here that all who sin and we all were born in sin, [18] are of their father the Devil. How can we be born again? We have to die! When we become dead-we die-the old sin nature within us dies—crucified on the cross! Paul says, *"It is no longer I who live, but Christ liveth in me."* [19] How do we die so we can give our bodies, mind, will and emotions to Christ? First of all, *"No man can come to Me, except the Father which hath sent Me draw him."* [20] God, through the Holy Spirit, draws us, and then God gives us repentance. [21] It is by REPENTANCE!

The Holy Spirit brings us to the place where we realize we are captive to sin, 'the good things we want to do, we don't do, and the bad things we don't want to do, we do.' We come to 'the knowledge of good and evil' by the law. [22] We understand we are doomed in life and in death; we are helpless to do anything about it, so we go to the only source of life and that is God through Jesus Christ. We *call* (the Greek word here means to invoke the power of someone greater than ourselves for something only they can do) upon Him, [23] and repent (feel sorry, grieve-sob desperately- as if to try to catch ones breath-over our sin, we have a change of heart about sin, come to hate sin as God does) and ask God to forgive us of sin. We SURRENDER (submit ourselves to the control of another) to Him because we understand that He died in our place to pay for our sin. The old man was crucified with Christ [24] over 2000 years ago when He poured out His life Blood. He became the Lamb and our scapegoat. He took upon Himself our sin and shed His blood as the atoning sacrifice for our sin. [25] We ask Him to live His life in us. God made Jesus who had no sin **to be sin for us**, so that in Jesus we might become the righteousness of God. [26] "*I am crucified* (dead) **with Christ**: *nevertheless I live, yet not I, but Christ liveth in me.*" [27] "*anyone who does not take his cross and follow Me is not worthy of Me.*" [28] *Then Jesus said to his disciples, "If anyone would come after Me,* **he must deny himself** *and take up his cross and follow Me. For whoever wants to save his life will lose it,* *but whoever loses his life for Me will find it."* [29] I realize that on the Cross Christ took my place (He stood condemned for my sin). I confess that I am a sinner and RENOUNCE my sinful life. I submit my life to Jesus and die to my 'self' rule so that He can live in me!

Let's look at what Jesus told Nicodemus in John chapter three about being saved. "*There was a man of the Pharisees, named Nicodemus, a ruler of the Jews: the same came to Jesus by night, and said to Him, "Rabbi, we know that Thou art a teacher come from God; for no man can do these miracles that Thou doest, except God be with him." Jesus answered and said to him, "Verily, verily, I say unto thee,* EXCEPT A MAN BE BORN AGAIN **he cannot see the kingdom of God.**" *Nicodemus saith unto Him, "How can a man be born when he is old? Can he enter the second time into his mother's womb and be born?" Jesus answered, "Verily, verily, I say to thee,* **except a man be** BORN OF WATER AND OF THE SPIRIT**, he cannot enter into the kingdom of God**. *That which is born of the flesh is flesh; and that which is born of the Spirit is spirit. Marvel not that I said to thee, 'You must be born again.'* [30] Notice what He says here '*That which is born of the flesh is flesh*, what does that mean? Then He said, *unless one is born of*

water and Spirit he cannot enter into the Kingdom of God. When we are naturally born, we are born in the flesh in water. Flesh also means carnal. These two words are used alternately in the Bible when talking about a person who lives for himself and the pleasures of this world i.e., a sinner. *"Or do you not know that as many of us as were baptized into Christ Jesus were baptized into His death? Therefore we were buried with Him through baptism into death, that just as Christ was raised from the dead by the glory of the Father, even so we also should walk in newness of life."* [31] Also in reference to Israel crossing the Red Sea, Paul says they were *"baptized unto Moses in the cloud and in the sea."* [32] *"And Moses said to the people, '"Fear ye not, stand still, and see the salvation of the LORD, which He shall shew to you to-day: for the Egyptians whom ye have seen to-day, ye shall see them again no more forever. The LORD shall fight for you, and ye shall hold your peace." And the LORD said unto Moses..... "But lift thou up thy rod, and stretch out thine hand over the sea and divide it: and the children of Israel shall go on dry ground through the midst of the sea."'* [33]
In other words we died to the old sin nature through repentance (we had a change of mind and heart about our lives and we want to be done with it, so we cry out (invoke-call) to the only one who can save us.) We bury that old sin nature in the waters of baptism and as we rise out of the water we are resurrected to live a new life. When you bury something it is out of sight. Egypt is a picture of sin and the bondage of sin over and over again throughout Scripture. Notice that the LORD tells Israel they will not see them again forever! Does that say anything to you about the sin nature and the freedom we have from it? He has removed our sin as far as the east is from the west! [34] (We quote that Scripture over and over yet still claim we are still controlled by the sin nature.) That can only be done by the Holy Spirit. When He says you must also be born of the Spirit to inherit eternal life, He also said that he who is born of the Spirit is spirit. Now what is spirit? Let's go back to the Garden of Eden. Remember God said, *"Let Us make man in Our image and in our likeness."* Remember what likeness means, <u>the quality or state of being like, appearance, resemblance, semblance, copy, etc.</u> In other words, God made Adam with His same nature and appearance; he was like HIM-plural. The only exception was His deity. Adam and Eve had the characteristics of God the Father, God the Son and the Holy Spirit originally. They were a copy of God the Father, God the Son and God the Holy Spirit. <u>They were body, soul and spirit.</u> I will take a little liberty here and use the analogy of God the Father being like the soul of man; mind, will and emotions: Jesus said, I have come to do <u>Your will</u>, O God. [35] *'And the LORD <u>was</u> <u>sorry</u> that He had made man*

on the earth, and He was <u>grieved</u> in His heart.' [36] *"For the LORD thy God is a consuming fire, even a <u>jealous</u> God."* [37] There are many other illustrations about the emotions and mind and will of God. God the Son is like the body of man, He was incarnate; *"He was made flesh and dwelt among us."* [38] And God the Holy Spirit is spirit; a spirit doesn't have flesh and bones. [39] *'Thus declares the LORD who stretches out the heavens, lays the foundation of the earth, and <u>forms the spirit of man within him</u>,* [40] and *"Rid yourselves of all the offenses you have committed, and get a new heart and <u>a new spirit</u>. Why will you die, O house of Israel?"* [41]

So what happened in the Garden of Eden? Remember when Adam and Eve had eaten of the fruit of the 'Tree of the Knowledge of Good and Evil,' it said when *'<u>God came walking</u>'* in the Garden in the cool of the day; *'they hid themselves'* because <u>they knew</u> they were naked.' [42] And God said, *"How did you know you were naked, didst thou eat from the tree in the midst of the garden?"* [43] Didn't God tell them that in the day they ate of the tree they would surely die? What died? Physically they did not immediately die, so what died? The soul of man did not die; they still had a will, intellect and emotions. The only explanation is that the spirit within them died. Spiritual death brings about separation from God. [44] They knew they were naked because the former glory (Spirit) of the Lord that they had been created with was now gone. They were 'defaced' of God's glory. (See 1 Samuel 4:21-22). They were no longer the glorious creatures God had made; they were now fleshly or carnal. Remember earlier I said it was as if they were *'clothed with the Spirit of God.'* Note also that it says they *"sewed fig leaves together and made themselves coverings"* [45] yet when God came walking they hid themselves because they were naked. This will give us a glimpse into how they were naked yet not ashamed in God's presence before sin; they had been clothed with the glory or Spirit of God. Yet now although they were clothed with fig leaves they felt naked. They were not physically naked but spiritually naked. They had been exposed! Just as when you or I are caught in disobedience and found out we feel guilt or we feel exposed. Our inner man is laid bare; that hidden act is out in the open. For further understanding about being clothed with the glory of God let's look at what 1 Corinthians 11:7 says concerning a person after receiving Jesus Christ as Savior, *'For a man indeed ought not to cover his head, <u>since he is the image and glory of God</u>....'* Here Paul is saying that man after receiving Jesus Christ as Savior; is once again 'clothed' with the glory of God. Now how can I say we were spiritually dead? *'<u>When you were dead</u> in your sins and in the uncircumcision of your sinful nature, <u>God made you alive</u> with Christ. He forgave us all our sins,'* [46] and *"Therefore,* *just as sin entered the world through one man, and <u>death through sin</u>, and in this way death came to all, because all sinned—."* [47] So we see here they did die, the spirit man died, because the Bible says that the spirit gives life.' *The <u>Spirit gives life</u>; the flesh counts for nothing.* **The words I have spoken to you are spirit and they are life.**' [48] Not only did they die immediately in spirit, but it also brought about a gradual death physically. The soul of man will never die; it will live eternally, for we were created eternal creatures in the image of an eternal God. The soul is the part of man that at the New Birth or Salvation is *BEING SAVED*. Let's look at Genesis 3:22 And the LORD God said, *"The man has now become like one of us, knowing good and evil. <u>He must not be allowed to reach out his hand and take also from the Tree of Life and eat, and live forever—</u>"* This is speaking of physically living forever. We note here man had not eaten from the Tree of Life, which if he had done so instead of the Tree of the Knowledge of Good and Evil, he would have remained in a state of physical eternal life on this earth. Now we are doomed to die physically, but if we receive Christ as our Savior we will be able to eat from the tree of life in heaven. [49] But for those who DO NOT receive Jesus Christ as their personal Savior, they will die physically and then experience greater spiritual death which is total absence of God's presence in hell.[50] Jesus said, *"I tell you the truth if you will listen to what I say and believe the One who sent Me you will have eternal life and will not be condemned but* **'has crossed over from death to life.'"** There will come a time when those who hear My voice will live. [51] Now if God was talking about immediate physical death in the Garden, what does Jesus mean in these Scriptures when He says whoever 'hears' or listens to what I say 'has crossed from death to life' and again 'the dead will hear and will live.' What does He mean 'whoever' <u>hears</u> My word and believes shall live? He is saying whoever is attentive and really listens to and believes, i.e., trust in what I say will have eternal life. *"For the one who sows to his own flesh will from the flesh reap <u>corruption</u>, but the one who sows to the Spirit will from the Spirit reap eternal life."* [52] Corruption according to Webster's means depravity, decay, and decomposition. What happens when you die? Your body decays, it decomposes! What is depravity? It's the activity of being depraved-perverted, corrupt or evil. *"And those who belong to Christ Jesus (the Messiah) have* **crucified the flesh** *(the godless human nature) with its passions and appetites and desires. If we live by the [Holy] Spirit, let us also walk by the Spirit. [If by the Holy Spirit we have our life in God, let us go forward walking in line, our conduct controlled by the Spirit.]* [53] What are the results of living by or sowing to the Spirit? You will began to see the Spirit manifest in your daily life or shall I say fruit of the Spirit. *"But the fruit of the [Holy] Spirit [the work which His presence within accomplishes] is love, joy (gladness), peace, patience (an even temper, forbearance), kindness, goodness (benevolence), faithfulness, Gentleness (meekness, humility), self-control (self-restraint, continence). Against such things there is no law [that can bring a charge].*[54]

SO HOW CAN I BE BORN AGAIN to escape death and hell?

*"For God so loved the world that He gave His only begotten Son, **that whoever believes** in Him shall not perish, but have eternal life. For God did not send the Son into the world to judge the world, but that the world might be saved through Him. He who **believes** in Him is not judged; he who does not believe has been judged already, because he has not **believed** in the name of the only begotten Son of God."* [55] *`But what does it say? "THE WORD IS NEAR YOU, in your mouth and in your heart"—that is, the word of faith which we are preaching, that if you **confess with your mouth** Jesus as Lord, and **believe in your heart** that God raised Him from the dead, you will be saved; for **with the heart** a person believes, **resulting in righteousness, and with the mouth he confesses, resulting in salvation**."'* [56] *"For while we were still helpless, at the right time Christ died for the ungodly. But God demonstrates His own love toward us, in that while we were yet sinners, Christ died for us."* [57]

Remember what John the Baptist and Jesus both preached to those who came for baptism? They both preached *"**Repent**, for the Kingdom of Heaven is at hand"* when calling people to receive the Gospel. What was the purpose of Repenting? What is repentance? We briefly discussed this earlier but here we give the true definitions from the Bible.

THERE ARE FOUR WORDS IN THE BIBLE FOR REPENTANCE, TWO IN HEBREW {OLD TESTAMENT} TWO IN GREEK {NEW TESTAMENT}

OLD TESTAMENT

> ***NACHAM*** *— (naw-kham')* to *sigh* i.e. *breathe* strongly; by implication To be sorry, To console, pity or rue, Lament, to grieve, to sigh, to groan. It literally refers to difficulty in breathing while experiencing intense emotion. (Exodus 32:12)

SHUWB– (*shoob*) TO TURN BACK, with the idea of turning back to the starting point, *To retreat, reverse, withdraw*-to make a radical change in attitude toward sin and God (1 Samuel 15:29)

NEW TESTAMENT-

METANOEO– (*met-an'-oy-ah*) *to think differently afterwards, i.e. reconsider,* to have another mind or change your mind & attitude toward sin (Matthew 4:17, Mark 6:12)

METAMELLOMAI– (*met-am-el'-lom-ahee*) to *care afterwards,* i.e. *regret:—*repent (Hebrews 7:21)

Another word closely relating to repentance is ***EPISTREPHO*** –(*ep-ee-stref'-o*) which means to come again, convert, (re)turn (about, again)-A spiritual transition from sin to God. (Luke 22:32)[58]

John the Baptist says to ***Repent*** and to the religious leaders (self righteous) he says, "bring ***fruit*** 'meet' for repentance." The word meet means there is evidence that you are sincere. As you can see from the previous mentioned definitions the *'fruit meet for repentance'* [59] is that which brings you to the place (by the convicting power of the Holy Spirit) that you are ready to do something about your sinful condition. You understand or acquire the knowledge that you are dead in trespasses and sin. You are no longer just sorry; you are grieved to the point of deep sobbing (difficulty in breathing) that you have offended a Holy God; you realize sin is a destructive force in your life and you are helpless to do anything about it, with all your heart you are ready for a change of actions to bring about different results. Therefore, you *'call' (invoke) upon the name of the Lord.* *"For whoever calls upon the name of the Lord shall be saved."* [60] CALL in the original text comes from the Greek word *ep-ee-kal-eh' which means to invoke* (for worship, testimony, decision, etc.) *to appeal to, to* call *on, upon.* It does not mean just to say the name in a prayer. When you call upon the Lord in Repentance you are invoking the power of His Majesty for Salvation, hence the part of the definition 'decision'; you have made a decision, a decision to turn AWAY FROM SIN and TURN TO HIM.

WHAT PART OF US IS TOUCHED BY REPENTANCE?

In James Lee Beall's book, *Laying a Foundation*, he states that "repentance changes four basic areas in us: ***emotion, will, intellect and spirit.*** It involves the complete transfer of our love and investment from sin and selfish aims to God." [61] Notice our body is not listed here, we may still have the same physical appetites that were present before repentance. When we accept Jesus Christ as our personal Savior, the Holy Spirit is in us. We are to be led by the Spirit through our spirit man and therefore we are to '*subdue*' our bodies. "*For if you live according to the flesh you will die; but if by the Spirit you **put to death** the deeds of the body, you will live.*" [62]

Just like the wheat that falls into the ground and dies that it may produce much grain, when we 'fall into Jesus' death and die, we are then resurrected into new life. [63] We are then to '*reckon ourselves dead indeed to sin and alive to God in Christ Jesus our Lord.*' [64] Reckon means to consider or regard, ***to determine by reference to a fixed basis*** or to settle accounts. Jesus is that fixed basis, we have determined by Jesus' death on the cross that '*He died once for all.*'[65] He took upon Himself my sin, sickness, disease, my confusion, disillusionment and my deadness in trespasses and sin and bore it on the cross. He gave me in return His righteousness, His healing, His soundness of mind, and His life. [66] We quit trying to be good enough or save ourselves by doing the right thing. We quit living for ourselves and quit trying to be our own god. We surrender; we give up and yield to Christ. We *let* ourselves die! What is the difference between trying and yielding or surrender? Trying is our effort to accomplish something on our own, yielding or surrendering is letting go and allowing it to be done in us and through us. This is a daily, moment by moment surrender. As we surrender moment by moment Scriptures says we are "*being transformed… from glory to glory.*" [67] We begin to produce more and more of the fruit of righteousness. Notice He gave me His righteousness! We cannot '*go on sinning,*'[68] because if we continue to sin after having receive Jesus as our Savior we 'crucify' Him all over again and bring shame to His name. [69] We were in Him on the Cross and our sin became His sin. When Christ died, we died! The old man, sin nature, old Adam, in us died! He died so that we would no longer live for our self but live for Him. We don't look at ourselves in the same way, that is, according to the worlds standard because '*IF anyone is in Christ, **he is a new creation; old things have passed away.***' [70] What do we say when a person dies? They have passed away! Hence the ***necessity of Baptism***-burying the old man (old things have DIED), **behold all things have become new**. We must be just as CONVINCED of this dying to the old sin nature as Eve was convinced in the Garden of Eden that the fruit was good for food, pleasant to the eyes and desirable to make one wise.

"Repent and let every one of you be baptized in the name of Jesus Christ for the remission (deliverance, pardon, liberty) *of sins; and you shall receive the Holy Spirit."* [71] What do we call a baby when it is born? We refer to them as new babies. Does the Word say that the spirit of man becomes new and everything else is the same? Did it say we have the same old nature to sin, and we're just forgiven for it? Did it say, "Well that old man is still alive but now we have a new nature too. They are going to battle it out?" (Think about this in the light of Adam and Eve sinning in the Garden-did they still have God's nature reigning in them.) NO! NO! NO! It says, "OLD THINGS HAVE **DIED** AND **ALL** THINGS HAVE BECOME NEW!" Is anything excluded in 'all'? NO! The word 'all' in Strong's means *thoroughly, whole, everything, whatsoever* or *whosoever* just like it does in English. You receive the Holy Spirit by which you can now live a new life. You receive the life of Christ within you. *"I do not pray for these* (apostles) *alone, but also **for those who will believe** in Me through their word; that they all may be one, as You, Father, are in Me and I in You; **that they also may be one in Us,** that the world may believe that You sent Me, **And the glory which You gave Me I have given them, that they may be one just as We are one:** I in them, and You in Me; **that they may be made perfect** in one, and that the world may know that You have sent Me, and have loved them as You have loved Me."* [72] Are God and Satan both in you battling for the upper hand in your life? Can Satan live with the glory of God in you? How can you or I be made perfect with Satan still in control most of the time? If you're still clinging to the old man i.e., that sin nature, (believing he is alive) he hasn't died yet! You see everything is by faith (trust). *"Without faith it is impossible to please Him, for he who comes to God **must believe** that He is, and that He is a rewarder of those who diligently seek Him."* [73] When one *believes*, just like the Spirit of God overshadowed Mary and Jesus was conceived in her, the Holy Spirit of God overshadows them and the Life of Jesus is conceived in them. He makes His abode within them. They are born of the Spirit. What was dead (the Spirit of God) has been made alive in them. Let's look at the new birth process like this: First, it is as if we're impregnated with conviction (guilt) by the Holy Spirit of our sin nature. Secondly, we labor (grieve with intense sorrow, try to catch our breath— sound like child birth) through repentance which brings forth Salvation— the third part of the process; faith (trusting in and relying on the death and

Christianity

resurrection of Christ). The whole process is from God. His Spirit convicts; [74] He grants us repentance [75] and then He gives us faith to believe. [76] God does the work; even supplying the faith for us to believe. When we take hold (receive by faith) what God has done the results are that *"we present our bodies <u>a living sacrifice</u> to God which is our reasonable service."* We no longer conform to this world, but we are transformed by the renewing of our minds. [77] Jesus says in Luke, if you want to follow Me you '**must deny yourself** and **take up your cross** <u>daily</u> and follow Me. Because if you want to keep living like you always have you will *DIE*, but if you will give up your life for Me you will save it. [78] Then again He says, *'yet to all who **received** Him, to those who **believed in His name**, He gave the <u>right</u> to become children of God—who were born, not of blood, nor of the will of the flesh, nor of the will of man, **but of God**.'* [79]

We are born again because of the will of God! Not because of anything we do or desire. AS A CHRISTIAN THE WORD SAYS WE ARE DEAD TO SIN AND ALIVE IN CHRIST! Look at Romans the sixth Chapter. I will paraphrase most of it. We will start with 5:21 because 6:1 ask a question in regards to chapter five. Just like *'sin reigned in death'*, so also *'grace might reign through righteousness'* so we will have eternal life through Jesus Christ our Lord. Should we keep sinning so grace will increase? '**NO WAY**! <u>We died to sin</u>;' so how can we keep living in sin? Don't you understand that when we were baptized into Christ we *'were baptized into his death?'* We were buried with Him in baptism and just like He was raised from the dead we were too by God's glory, so we will live a new life. Because *'If'* we were one with Him in death we will certainly be one with Him in His resurrection. *'For we <u>know</u> that <u>our old self was crucified</u> with Him so that <u>the body of sin might be done away with</u>, that we should no longer be slaves to sin— because anyone who has died has been <u>freed from sin</u>'.* What does anything dead do? Nothing! Because it's dead! What does it mean to 'do away' with something? It means to get rid of it. It is no longer in your possession. Paul reiterates this by saying in verse seven of chapter six that one has been 'freed' or liberated from sin. You are no longer its slave. It cannot **control** you any longer unless you by choice allow it to. **We died with Christ** so we believe that we will live with Him. We understand that Christ was raised from the dead and will never die again because death doesn't control Him anymore. When He died, He died once for all time and for all sin. He now lives for God. So now *<u>consider yourselves to be dead</u> <u>as far as sin is concerned,</u>* and *consider yourselves to be alive as far as God is concerned.* [80] The King James and New King James versions say *'Reckon'* instead of 'consider' yourselves dead to sin. The word, reckon means, as previously stated, to settle accounts, to determine by reference to a fixed basis. You have settled your account with God. Christ died for you: He became sin for you.[81] You have come to Him as your ADVOCATE (one that pleads the cause of another before a tribunal or court); you **by faith** have received what He did for you. Christ is the 'fixed' bases for your sin. His death 'fixed' the problem of the sin nature in your life. Jesus Christ killed (crucified) the nature of sin on the Cross and in you. You are no longer broken by sin. Christ has pled your case before God the Father. You receive it by faith. '**So don't let sin rule your body. Don't obey its evil longings. Don't give the parts of your body to serve sin. Don't let them be used to do evil. Instead, give yourself to God. You have been brought from death to life. Give the parts of your body to Him to do what is right. SIN WILL NOT BE YOUR MASTER!** The law does not rule you. God's grace has set you free. Should we sin because we are not ruled by law but by God's grace? Not at all**! Don't you know that when obey someone you become that person's slave**? If you want to be a slave to sin you will die. Or you can obey God and live a godly life. You used to be a slave of sin. But thank God that **you obeyed God with your <u>whole heart</u>**! And now **<u>you have been set free from sin.</u>** Because you are now <u>slaves</u> to right living. I know this is hard to understand because you are thinking like a man, but I am trying to help you comprehend that you don't need keep using your eyes, ears, mouth and other parts of your body to sin. Clean up your life and begin to live right, and do not keep becoming more and more evil. Give your bodies as a sacrifice to right living so you will become holy. You used to be a slave of sin and right living did not control you. What did you gain from that? Aren't you ashamed of how you used to live? Those things you used to do only led to death. [82] When you gave yourself to Jesus Christ, the sentence of the curse was broken and you are now controlled by the 'law of the Spirit' and are alive because of what Jesus did. *It has set you free from the law of sin that brings death. <u>Now you can do everything the law requires</u>*." [83] The sinful nature no longer controls the way you live. The Holy Spirit now controls the way you live. You are now a slave to God.

Earlier I quoted Colossians 2:13 which says; '*When you were dead in your sins and in the uncircumcision of your sinful nature, God made you alive with Christ. He forgave us ALL our sins,*' Let's look at the 'uncircumcision of your sinful nature'. Paul is using circumcision as a reference to the covenant God had made with Israel. Circumcision was ordained of God as a sign of 'covenant relationship' with God. It was a lasting covenant, one that held grave consequences if not adhered to. One could not participate in the Feast of the LORD nor make sacrifices if he were not circumcised. If you or your children were not circumcised, it was rebellion in the eyes of God. We see this in Exodus where Moses was on his way to Egypt to deliver the people of Israel. It says, *"And it came to pass by the way in the inn, that the LORD met him* (Moses) *and sought to kill him. Then Zipporah took a sharp stone and cut off the foreskin of her son and cast it at Moses; feet, and said, 'Surely a bloody husband art thou to me!'"* [84] God had explicitly stated that every male child was to be circumcised and those that were not would *'be cut off from his people for he has broken My covenant.'* [85] Moses had failed to circumcise his son, thereby breaking the covenant of God and bringing judgment upon himself. Cut off means die! God was going to kill him! We see this again in Joshua, where all the men who had left Egypt had to be circumcised before entering into Canaan because none of them had been circumcised in the wilderness. *"Then the Lord said to Joshua, 'This day I have rolled away the reproach of Egypt from you.'"* [86] I must interject here: the 'reproach' or guilt of Egypt has been rolled away-this is a picture of God 'taking away' guilt of sin. We see in this that God does not change, because now through our death, burial and resurrection *by faith* we have the same covenant of circumcision, but now it is circumcision of the heart. *"In Him you were also circumcised with the circumcision made without hands,* **by putting off the body of the sins of the flesh***, by the circumcision of Christ, buried with Him in baptism, in which you also were raised with Him through faith in the working of God, who raised Him from the dead."* [87] *"A man is not a Jew if he is only one outwardly, nor is circumcision merely outward and physical. No, a man is a Jew if he is one inwardly; and circumcision is **circumcision of the heart, by the Spirit**, not by the written code. Such a man's praise is not from men, but from God."* [88] What we could not do by natural means Christ has done by our faith, He by our obedience in repentance and obedience in baptism, has cut away the evil "foreskin" of our heart that held us in bondage to sin. In Hebrews 10: 1-2, the writer is speaking with the Jews concerning their faith in Christ and how Christ fulfilled the law of God. *"<u>For the law</u>, having a <u>shadow</u> of the good things to come, and not the very image of the things, <u>can never</u> with these same sacrifices which they offer continually year by year, <u>make those who approach perfect</u>. <u>For then would they not have ceased to be offered?</u> **<u>For the worshippers once purified, would have had no more consciousness of sins</u>**."* Note: first of all the underlined words-*'the law can never make those who approach perfect'* and secondly *'the worshippers <u>once purified</u>'*–Jesus died *'for sin once for all,'* [89] they *'would have no more consciousness of sins'* [90] – consciousness or awareness, perception of sin. There would be *"Therefore, there is now no condemnation* 'of 'sin' *of those who are in Christ Jesus."* [91] Why? Because Christ Jesus is in us and we are in Him. [92] *"He became our sin that we would become the righteousness of God in Him,"* [93] and because we *"walk not after the flesh* (carnal desires, sin) *but after the Spirit,"* [94] Our evil heart was circumcised, cutting away that sinful 'flesh' nature, (you can't undo a circumcision), and now we have a heart not dull and hardened by sin (like scar tissue) but soft and pliable, to receive the engrafted Word (Jesus). We now can rise to newness of life without the nature to sin constantly hanging over us, condemning us.

SO WHAT IS BEING BORN AGAIN? Your spirit man was dead because of the sin nature you inherited from your father Adam. But because you heard the Word of God and responded to it with repentance calling upon the *Name of God*-**Jesus Christ** for Salvation, you died to the old man, He (Jesus) raised you to new life and put His Spirit within you, and you are now alive spiritually. Because the Spirit of God is within you, you separate yourself from the world, i.e. the world's ideas, philosophies and desires. You are separated unto God; which is the process of sanctification (being made holy having been set apart for a sacred purpose). You are set apart to God to fulfill His purposes in the earth. In the prayer we know as 'The Lord's Prayer,' the second verse or phrase is "Thy kingdom come in the earth as it is in heaven." [95] We are in essence asking God to bring about His will THROUGH US in the earth. *"Because ye are sons, God sent the Spirit of His Son into your hearts, crying, Abba, Father."* [96] He tells us to come out from the world system and to separate ourselves from it. Don't touch what is unclean and I will receive you. I will be your Father and you will be My children. Because we have these promises, **'let us purify ourselves from everything that contaminates body and spirit, perfecting holiness out of reverence for God.'** [97] Do not grieve the Holy Spirit of God [98] by continuing to walk in sin. When you continue in sin you, *"crucify again the Son of God, and put Him to an open shame"* [99] because *"He who sins is of the devil….."* [100] The word 'sins' is plural signifying continually sinning or practicing sin. But we are to *"make our calling and election sure…"* [101] for we must be born again!

Christianity

CHAPTER TEN

[1] John 3:6-7[5]
[2] James 1:18 [5]
[3] John 3:3
[4] Titus 3:5[5]
[5] Genesis 21:1-7
[6] Matthew 13:11
[7] John 12:23-26[8]
[8] Romans 6:2-7 [4]
[9] John 8:44, Matthew 13:37 & 39
[10] Romans 6:2-3
[11] 1Peter 1:3[4]
[12] John 1:13[5]
[13] 1Peter 1:23[4]
[14] 1John 2:29[4]
[15] John 8:31-36[8]
[16] John 8:44[4]
[17] Matthew 13:37 & 39
[18] Romans 3:23
[19] Galatians 2:20
[20] John 6:44
[21] 2 Timothy 2:25
[22] Romans 7:19
[23] Romans 10:13
[24] Romans 6:6
[25] Leviticus 16 & Hebrews 9:11-28
[26] 2Corinthians 5:21
[27] Galatians 2:20
[28] Matthew 10:38[5]
[29] Matthew 16:24 & 25[5]
[30] John 3:1-7
[31] Romans 6: 3, 4[8] also see 1 Peter 3:18, 21
[32] 1 Corinthians 10:2
[33] Exodus 14:13-16
[34] Psalm 103:8
[35] Hebrews 10:9
[36] Genesis 5: 6[8]
[37] Deuteronomy 4:24
[38] John 1:14

[39] Luke 24:39
[40] Zechariah 12:1[4]
[41] Ezekiel 18:31[5]
[42] Genesis 3:8, 10
[43] Genesis 3:11
[44] Isaiah 59:2
[45] Genesis 3:7
[46] Colossians 2:13[5]
[47] Romans 5:12[4]
[48] John 6:63[5]
[49] Revelations 22:14
[50] Revelation 21:8
[51] John 5:24-25
[52] Galatians 6:8[4]
[53] Galatians 5:24-25[1]
[54] Galatians 5:22-23[1]
[55] John 3:16-18
[56] Romans 10:8-10[6]
[57] Romans 5:6-8[4]
[58] OT #7725, #5162 and NT #3340, #3338 and #1994[13]
[59] Matthew 3:1, 2, 8
[60] Romans 10:13
[61] page 13[9]
[62] Romans 8:13[8]
[63] Hebrews 9:12
[64] Romans 6:11[8]
[65] Hebrews 10:10
[66] 2 Corinthians 5:21
[67] 2 Corinthians 3:18
[68] 1 John 3:4-9
[69] Hebrew 6:6
[70] 2 Corinthians 5:15-17
[71] Acts 2:38
[72] John 17:20-23
[73] Hebrews 11:6
[74] John 16:8
[75] 2 Timothy 2:25
[76] Romans 12:3
[77] Romans 12:1-2
[78] Luke 9:23-24

[79] John 1:12-13
[80] Romans 6:8-11
[81] 2 Corinthians 5:21
[82] Romans 6:6-21
[83] Romans 8:1, 2 & 4
[84] Exodus 4:24, 25
[85] Genesis 17:10-14
[86] Joshua 5:9
[87] Colossians 2:11-12
[88] Romans 2:29 [8]
[89] Hebrews 10:10[8]
[90] Hebrews 10:2
[91] Romans 8:1
[92] John 17:21-23 & Ephesians 2:6
[93] 2 Corinthians 5:21
[94] Romans 8:4
[95] Matthew 6:10
[96] Galatians 4:6
[97] 2 Corinthians 6:17-7:1
[98] Ephesians 4:30
[99] Hebrews 6:6
[100] 1 John 1:8
[101] 2 Peter 1:10

Chapter Eleven
What is faith?

According to Paul, *"Faith is the substance of things hoped for, the evidence of things not seen."* [1a] or *"Faith is being sure of what we hope for. It is being certain of what we do not see"*. [1b] The New Living Translation says it this way: ***"Faith is the confidence that what we hope for will actually happen; it gives us the assurance about things we cannot see"***.

Webster's Dictionary defines <u>FAITH</u> as confidence, trust, belief, reliance, trustworthiness and persuasion, and <u>SUBSTANCE</u> as the ultimate reality that underlies all outward manifestations and change. In essence faith is simply **Trust**. Notice that substance is ***<u>the ultimate reality that causes the outward manifestations and changes</u>***. What is the ultimate reality that we are talking about? OUR SALVATION! The word ultimate means: last in progression, final, eventual extreme, utmost. And it's a Reality! (Remember earlier I said we are BEING saved) And because of this ultimate reality (our Salvation) it produces in us MANIFESTATIONS (a public demonstration of power and purpose) and change!!! We are no longer the same! Something has happened that we may not immediately see physically, but it will bring about a personality change. Behold all things become new! Become-a process, we are becoming new! We are no longer 'just sinners' saved by grace. We are new creations in Christ Jesus! We are recreated in Christ Jesus. God, as it were through Salvation, gives us a heart transplant. He takes out the old, dead, sin diseased heart and gives us a new one. **The sinner died! We are alive in Christ Jesus!** That is *the light* of the Gospel of the Glory of Christ!! [2] Therefore, ***"Let us keep <u>looking</u>** to Jesus. He is the author of faith. <u>He also makes it perfect.</u>*

He paid no attention to the shame of the cross. He suffered there because of the joy He was looking forward to. Then He sat down at the right hand of the throne of God." [3] 'Looking' in the Greek according to Strong's Concordance is, ap-ob-lep'-o which means to look away from everything else in order to look intently on one object. The object of our faith-**God!**

OSWALD CHAMBERS IN <u>*MY UTMOST FOR HIS HIGHEST*</u>, states it this way, "Faith is not intelligent understanding, <u>faith is deliberate commitment</u> to a Person where I see no way." ' [4]

WHAT IS FAITH'S ROLE IN SALVATION?

Paul says in Romans, ***"for I am not ashamed of the gospel of Christ, for it is the power of God to Salvation for everyone who <u>believes</u>, ...for in <u>it</u>** (the Gospel) **the righteousness of God is revealed from faith to faith; ... the just shall live by <u>faith</u>."*** [5] Faith is the key that unlocks the door to Salvation. Jesus said, *"Behold I stand at the door and knock, if anyone hears My voice and opens the door, I will come in to him, and dine with him, and he with Me."* [6] Faith is not only the key that unlocks the door; it is the key that opens the door. It allows the power of the resurrection of Jesus to come into our hearts and raise us from the dead. Faith is not faith until acted upon. Only when we are convinced of something do we act upon it. If we truly believe that we are spiritually raised to newness of life, that the old life is gone and the new life has come, we will think differently, talk differently and walk differently. Our perspective of life will change. When you see the word faith, think trust! If we trust something, we are not hesitant concerning it! It produces confidence! We become confident that our old sin nature is gone and Jesus Christ has given us a new nature-a nature like His, displaying His holiness.

CHAPTER ELEVEN

[1] Hebrews 1: 1 1a-8, 1b-7
[2] 2 Corinthians 4:4
[3] Hebrews 12:2
[4] March 28 devotion
[5] Romans 1:16-17
[6] Revelation 3:20

Chapter Twelve

Walking After The Spirit Not After The Flesh

A study of Romans chapters seven and eight will give greater understanding of walking after the Spirit and not after the flesh. Just as Jesus used parables to explain Kingdom Principles, in chapter seven of Romans Paul is explaining our relationship to the law verses our relationship to Christ through an analogy of marriage. *"Know ye not, brethren (for I speak to those who know the law how that the law hath dominion over a man as long as he liveth? For the woman which hath a husband is bound by the law to her husband so long as he liveth; but if the husband be dead, she is loosed from the law of her husband. So then if, while her husband liveth, she be married to another man, she will be called an adulteress; but if her husband be dead, she is free from that law; so that she is no adulteress, though she be married another man."* [1] Paul, in Romans chapter six, has just told the Roman church that they had died to sin in verse two, and were buried in the waters of baptism, that sin was no longer their master, that they should 'reckon' themselves dead to sin in verse eleven of chapter six. They should not present their members (body) as instruments of sin in verse thirteen of six, because they were no longer under law but under grace in verse fourteen of the same chapter. He goes on to expound that whomever you obey you are their slave and are in bondage to in verses 15-23 of six. Now in chapter seven Paul is explaining through the example of marriage that they are no longer subject to the dominion of the Law because they died to sin and they buried it in Christ. In verse four he explains that they are now *"dead to the law through the body of Christ, that we may be married to another—-to Him ... that they should bear fruit to God."* In verses five and six of chapter seven he summarizes chapter six and first portion of chapter seven. In verses seven through twelve he is showing that the only way we knew how sinful we were is by the law. That is how sin became exceedingly sinful. The law exposed sin; before I understood what sin was I seemed to be ok, but when I finally knew what sin was, it came alive and I died. It was as if understanding what sin was brought death to me. In verses thirteen through twenty-three Paul uses himself as an example of living under the law trying to do what is right and not being able to, and yet when trying not do what is wrong , doing it anyway. It is an analogy of the frustration of trying to obey the law in the flesh. Paul is simply stating the controlling nature of sin; he is not saying he is still in bondage to it, but he is merely explaining how it works through the law. (Why would he be so adamant in chapter six about being dead to sin and being free from it and then confessing in chapter seven that he still had no power over it?) In verse twenty-four of seven he asks where deliverance is, and answers the question in verse twenty-five through *"Jesus Christ our Lord! So then <u>with the mind I myself</u> serve the law of God <u>but with the flesh the law of sin</u>."* Paul is saying is that our deliverance from the bondage of the law and sin can only come through Jesus Christ. We by our understanding try to serve the law of God but the flesh rises up and we serve the law of sin. He goes on to say in Romans chapter eight that we are not under condemnation *IF* we walk after the Spirit because we have been made FREE from *the law of sin and death,* verse two. God condemned sin in the flesh and through the death of Jesus Christ. He did what we could not do in ourselves, which is be free from sin following the law. If we walk after the <u>Spirit we will fulfill the righteous requirements of the law;</u> verse four. He continues, showing what it is to be 'walking' in the flesh and what it is to 'walk' in the Spirit; what your thoughts are concerned with is where you are. Either you are born of the Spirit, or you are still in bondage to the sin nature. If you are still walking after the lust of the flesh you are at war with God; you are not, nor can you be, obedient to God. Verse thirteen states that; *"If you live according to the flesh **you will die; but if you by the Spirit put to death the body, you will live**."* You cannot continue to fulfill the desire of the flesh and be 'saved,' because you are living against the very nature of God within you that you received when you were baptized. [2] Let's look at the baptism of Jesus to help us see what happened at our baptism. *"Then Jesus came from Galilee to John at the Jordan to be baptized by him. And John tried to prevent Him, saying, "I need to be baptized* *by You, and are You coming to me?" But Jesus answered and said to him, "Permit it to be so now, for thus it is fitting for us to fulfill all righteousness." Then he allowed Him. When He had been baptized, Jesus came up immediately from the water; and behold, the heavens were opened to Him, and He saw the Spirit of God descending like a dove and alighting on Him. And suddenly a voice came from heaven, saying, "This is My beloved Son, in whom I am well pleased."* [3] We are baptized, representing the death and burial of the sin nature, and we should, when rising up out of baptismal water, receive the Holy Spirit that gives us the power to walk in newness of life. [4] This has not been taught doctrinally in any church I have been associated with. I have been taught we are sealed with the Holy Spirit[5] or kept held in God's hand until we die and get to heaven or as a guarantee or down payment of what we will receive later (I'm not sure how much later, but by what I've been told not until the next life). But if we look further at the account of Jesus we see that He was led by the Holy Spirit into the wilderness to be tempted. He was tempted in every way we are tempted,[6] the lust of the flesh – food, the lust of the eyes – all the kingdoms of the world and the pride of life – 'jump and God will save you'. [7] When we rise from the waters of Baptism we are to be led by the Holy Spirit. [8] Yes Satan will still tempt us with all those things. But if we, like Jesus, will use the Scripture as the Sword of the Spirit, [9] we can overcome. [10] <u>That, my friend, is the power of the gospel of Christ to Salvation Paul is talking about in Romans 1:16</u>. If we do not receive the knowledge of the truth and continue to walk as if nothing happened except 'now we are sealed,' kept by God until the next life, we are being deceived by Satan and in danger of being cast into hell by ignorance and disobedience. *"But I fear that, as the serpent deceived Eve by his craftiness,* **your minds may be <u>corrupted</u> from the simplicity that is in Christ."** [11] **"*For if the message spoken by angels was binding, and every violation and disobedience received its just punishment,<u> how shall we escape if we ignore such a great salvation</u>?** *This salvation, which was first announced by the Lord, was confirmed to us by those who heard him."*[12] As Paul says in Galatians, *'If while I seek to be justified by Christ, I am found a sinner, is Christ a minister of sin? Certainly not!'* (So while I claim to be a Christian and I continue to walk in sin, I'm saying Christ is a minister of sin!) *'For if I build again those things which I destroyed, I make myself a transgressor.* (If I continue to live like I still have the old sin nature, I am transgressing against my Salvation. What I am saying is that the blood of Jesus was not enough to save me from sin.) *'For I through the law I died to the law that I might live unto God.'* (I died to the old man-that sin nature-that I might live unto God) *'I have been* *crucified with Christ'* (I was buried with Christ in baptism, so I must have died; I identified with His death on the cross.) *It is no longer I who lives,* (I died and was buried; you don't bury someone who is not dead) *but Christ that lives in me; and the life which I now live in the flesh, I live by faith in the Son of God, who loved me and gave Himself up for me.*[13] Paul says in 1 Corinthians. *"But someone will say, 'How are the dead raised up? And with what body do they come? Foolish one, **what you sow is not made alive unless it dies**? **And what you sow, you do not sow that body that shall be**,* (you sow a dead corrupt sin nature, and are raised to newness of life i.e. the righteousness of Christ Jesus)[14] *.....So also is the resurrection of the dead. The body is sown in corruption, it is raised in incorruption. It is sown in dishonor, it is raised in glory. It is sown in weakness, it is raised in power.*[15] Can you see the correlation to Romans six on the discussion on Baptism and the Parable of the Sower (mentioned in a previous chapter), and how we are raised to newness of life? *"Therefore, my beloved brethren, be steadfast, immovable, always abounding in the work of the Lord, know that your labor is not in vain in the Lord."*[16] Here, Paul is saying that we must put off corruption, or to quit walking in sin. We cannot walk in corruption and incorruption at the same time. If you are corrupt you cannot inherit the Kingdom of God. Romans 5:17 says, *"For if by the transgression of the one, death reigned through the one, MUCH MORE those who receive the abundance of grace and of the gift of righteousness will **REIGN IN LIFE** through the One, Jesus Christ."* What does it mean to reign? The original word in Greek is *basileuo-to rule (lit. or fig.) king, reign, it comes from bas-il-yooce' which means (through the notion of a foundation of power), a sovereign—king.* [17] The New Living Translation says it this way: *"For the sin of this one man, Adam, caused death to rule over many. But even greater is God's wonderful grace and His gift of righteousness, for all who receive it will live in triumph **over sin and death** through this one man, Jesus Christ."*

CHAPTER TWELVE

[1] Romans 7:1-3
[2] 1 John 3:8,9
[3] Matthew 3:13-17[8]
[4] Romans 6:4
[5] 2 Corinthians 1:22, Ephesians 4:30
[6] Matthew 4:1, 1 John 2:15
[7] Hebrews 4:15
[8] Romans 8:2
[9] Hebrews 4:12
[10] Revelations 2:7, 17,26: 3:5, 12 & 21
[11] 2 Corinthians 11:3 & Genesis 3:4
[12] Hebrews 2:2-3
[13] Galatians 2:17-21
[14] 1 Corinthians 15:35-37a
[15] 1 Corinthians 15:42-43
[16] 1 Corinthians 15:58
[17] *# 936, from 935*[6]

Chapter Thirteen

Eternal Security

Is the doctrine of eternal security taught in Scripture? Hebrews 7:25 says, *"Wherefore He is able also to save them to the uttermost that come unto God by Him, seeing He ever liveth to make intercession for them."* And Jude 24 & 25 says, *"Now unto Him that is able to keep you from falling, and to present you faultless before the presence of His glory with exceeding joy, To the only wise God our Savior, be glory and majesty, dominion and power, both now and ever."* I have been told by many who have no fruit of repentance in their lives that they are saved and when I ask how they know, they reply, "I made a profession of faith or I have accepted Christ as my Savior," or they may say, "I've been baptized or I belong to 'such and such' church." But when I ask them about sin in their lives they reply, "We're going to sin every day, we can't help it! Just because we're saved doesn't mean we're perfect." Another one I've heard used by many clergy, "Since becoming a Christian I now have two natures, the old sin nature and the new nature. They are at war with in me, each trying to control." An explanation given is the doctrine 'once saved-always saved' which I would like to explore for the sake of truth. Because the Bible itself says to let every word be established from two or more witnesses [1] we will look at the three Scriptures used for the basis of this doctrine and study them within the context from which they are taken. In seeing constant failure to meet the perfection of God in their lives, many, when falling short feel they must have two natures residing in them! And many feel as if the enemy is still has control and they cannot live above sin, and that they are, in essence, helpless to do anything about it! But, if that is true, then Jesus did not *TAKE AWAY THE SIN OF THE WORLD*, [2] His blood sacrifice does not have **the power** [3] the Bible states it does, we are truly without hope in this world, and Jesus is a liar! We have no need of the Bible because it cannot do what it claims to do!

Here are the Scriptures given as the basis for this doctrine: *"But what does it say? The word is near you, in your mouth and in your heart-that is, the word of faith which we are preaching, that if you <u>confess with your mouth</u> Jesus as Lord, and believe in your heart that God raised Him from the dead, <u>you will be saved;</u>"* [4] *"<u>For whoever will call on the name of the Lord will be saved</u>."* [5] *"And I give eternal life to them, and they will never perish; <u>and no one is able to snatch them out of the Father's hand.</u>"* [6]

SO LET'S LOOK AT THESE SCRIPTURES:

Each one of these Scriptures can be taken (out of context) to express exactly what has been claimed: 'Once saved, always saved.' Let's look at them within the context of the subject they are referring to along with some other scriptures I share after this. The first one, Romans 10:8-9, Paul begins the chapter telling his Roman audience that his heart's desire is for Israel to be saved. But they have rejected Christ and have a righteousness of their own that is through the Law of Moses. But the righteousness of <u>FAITH</u> is what he is preaching. Generally, when using these verses, the following verse is not quoted, but it explains why you are saved by confession and belief, *"For with the heart one <u>BELIEVES</u> <u>unto</u> <u>righteousness</u> and with the mouth <u>CONFESSION IS MADE</u> <u>unto</u> <u>salvation</u>."* [7] Now let's look at a very important word within the context of this scripture. (Unto-*preposition*-until+*to*) 'To'-*adverb*-used as a function word **to indicate a direction toward.** [8] In other words *heart faith* **causes one to move toward salvation and righteousness**. The believer is not resigned to sin and the sin nature; but by the *power of salvation* they begin to implement righteous acts with the help of the Holy Spirit. What is righteousness? (Righteous-*adjective*- acting rightly, upright, arising from an outraged sense of justice or morality.) [9]

Now let's look at Romans 10:13, *"Whoever will call on the name of the Lord will be saved."* The word 'calls' in this text is from the Greek word *ep-ee-kal-eh'* which means *to invoke* (for aid, worship, testimony, decision an appeal.) [10] It doesn't mean just to say the name of the Lord in a prayer. It means you are desperate for Him to do something for you, He's your only means of rescue, you are invoking Him for Salvation, you need Him to do something you are incapable of doing for yourself; you are in sin and cannot save yourself, and you need Him to SAVE you. You trust Him to reach out and take hold of you. TO TAKE YOU OUT OF

WHERE YOU ARE AND PUT YOU IN A PLACE OF SAFETY. You've made a decision recognizing that you are guilty of gross sin and you want God to do something! Let's look at it this way: You're in a pool, (sin i.e. the world) drowning, and you see the Lifeguard (Jesus); you cry (call) out for Him to save you. The lifeguard (Jesus) jumps into the pool (sin-He became sin for us [111]), takes hold of you, and pulls you to safety. Does he leave you in the pool (sin)? No; He takes you out of the pool (sin) and puts you in a place of safety. *"He has rescued us from the domain of darkness and transferred us to the kingdom of His beloved Son."* [12] The King James Version states it this way, *"Who hath delivered us from the power of darkness, and had translated us into the kingdom of His dear Son."* Translated means to bear or change from one place, state, form or appearance to another: TRANSFER, TRANSFORM. [13] After the Lifeguard takes you out of the pool (remember you were drowning-a lifeguard doesn't rescue you until you've exhausted every effort to save yourself), he doesn't just lay you on the ground and walk off. He begins to resuscitate you. What does he do? He does compression to expel the water, 'sin', from your lungs-that stops the life giving flow of oxygen (taking away of sin). When and only when the water is expelled can He then breathe the breath of life back into your lungs (the infilling of the life of God or the Holy Spirit). Jesus told Nicodemus in John 3:3, *"YOU MUST BE BORN AGAIN!"* Something takes place when you're born again. IT IS NOT JUST MAKING A COMMITMENT. IT IS NOT JUST ACKNOWLEDGING THAT JESUS IS LORD. Something happens deep inside your inner man; <u>you become different</u> i.e., a new creation, Jesus transforms and transfers you. Jesus Christ has placed His Spirit within you, the Holy Spirit! *"Therefore, if any man be in Christ, he is **a new creature: old things are passed away;** behold all things are become new."* [14] What does the term 'passed away' imply? It is a phrase that is used of someone who has 'died'. A NEW CREATURE! He recreated you! Behold <u>ALL</u> things are BECOME new! Whew! Glory to God! Praise be to God! I am no longer just a sinner saved by grace; I am a NEW CREATURE! Now, you can *draw back*, or *'backslide'*, go back and dig up that old dead nature and walk around in dead man's bones if you want too. You can jump back into the pool (sin, world); after all, 'that's where your friends are'. If you love that old life and just can't seem to 'put to death the deeds of the body' — *'If you are living according to the flesh, you must die!'* [15] *"Behold then the kindness and severity of God; on those who fell, severity, but to you, God's kindness, **IF** you continue in His kindness; <u>OTHERWISE YOU ALSO WILL BE CUT OFF</u>,"* [16] just as a branch that does not produce fruit is cut off from the vine and burned. [17]

Ok, now let's look at John 10:28. In the previous verses of John ten, Jesus is talking to the Jews. They are asking Him to plainly tell them whether or not He is 'THE' Christ (The Anointed One or Messiah). He replies, verse 26-28: "*But <u>you do not believe because you are not of My sheep</u>,*"... *My sheep hear My voice and I know them, and they <u>follow</u> Me; and I give eternal life to them, and they will never perish; and no one will snatch them out of My hand.*" How do you get to be a sheep? '<u>You are born into</u> the sheepfold!' And note the phrase 'snatch them out of My hand.' No one can take by force anyone out of Jesus' hand. **It does not** say no one can fall away, nor does it say that one can sin all the time and he WILL NOT go to hell! **It does not** refer to those who of their own volition (will) either turn away from the truth or because of willfulness continue to walk in known sin. **It is not** referring to those who '*hide iniquity in their heart*',[18] or those who refuse to give up some secret/or not so secret sin. Sin, again, is anything contrary to holiness, or anything that is a violation of God's truth. What it is saying is that no one can snatch- *har-pad'-zo*; (which the root word means to *take for oneself*) to *seize, to pluck, pull, take by force.* [19] You cannot be taken by force from God; you can, however, of your own willful disobedience fall from grace. "*Blessed is the man who <u>endures</u> temptation; <u>for when he has been approved</u>, he will receive the crown of life* .....[20] As it is stated in James we are tempted by our own lust or desire, God does not tempt us, but that desire once acted upon brings forth death. [21] When we look at this, we can see no one is seized or has taken by force the one tempted. It was a decision made on the part of the one tempted. Who did the tempting? The lust/desire of the one tempted; *<u>his own desire</u>* drew him away. *Desire* in the New King James is the same word as *lust* in the King James of this particular portion of Scripture. So we see here that no other entity was involved in the snatching away. The one who sinned is at fault. WE ARE GIVEN THE RIGHT, PRIVILEGE, AND AUTHORITY TO BECOME THE CHILDREN OF GOD.[22] Just as Adam was given the right, privilege and authority to subdue the earth, but did not exercise that right, privilege and authority when facing the serpent in the Garden of Eden. Remember the word 'Let' earlier referred to. (There is a whole lot riding on the word 'let', so in studying scripture make note of the verbs.) ONLY AS WE EXERCISE THE RIGHT, POWER AND AUTHORITY, DO WE RECEIVE THE ADOPTION AS SONS.

"*You He <u>made alive</u>, who were dead, in trespasses and sins,*"[23] Notice the 'were' that is past tense, meaning there has been a change. "*When you <u>were</u> dead in your transgressions and the uncircumcision of your flesh, He made you alive together with Him, having forgiven us all our transgressions, <u>having canceled out</u> the certificate of debt consisting of decrees* *against us, which was hostile to us; and* **He has taken it out of the way, having nailed it to the cross.**" [24] One translation uses the word <u>obliterated</u> instead of canceled out. What does it mean that Jesus '*having taken it out of the way, having nailed it to the cross?*' What has He taken out of the way? What is/was the certificate of our debt? Our SIN! How does that keep me from sinning every day? Well, what does it mean when you take something away? If your child has something that they don't need or that you prefer them not to have and you take it away, do they still possess it? **No!** They no longer have control over it! Jesus nailed our sin to the Cross. Did it come down when they took Him off the Cross and jump back on us? NO! NO! A thousand times No! The same principle applies here. I may be getting a little deep for some of you but hang on! **WE BECOME DEAD TO SIN AND ALIVE TO CHRIST JESUS**.

Look with me at Hebrews the tenth chapter, please read the whole chapter. I'll quote verse thirty-nine here: *"But we are not of those* **who draw back to perdition**, *but of those who* <u>believe</u> **to the saving of the soul**." What does it mean to draw back to perdition? Webster defines perdition as: utter destruction, loss, eternal damnation. [25] Strong's Concordance defines it as: ruin or loss (physically, spiritually, or eternal) destruction, die. [26] This word is taken from the root word that means to destroy fully. The devil is called the son of perdition. Verse thirty-eight says, *"Now the just shall live by faith; But if anyone* **draws back**, *My soul has no pleasure in Him."* What does it mean to '*draw back*'? Draw is an "'*intransitive verb*' meaning to move in a particular direction, often alongside, toward or away from something else, and with a smooth steady motion." [27] So it means to make a smooth steady motion back to the place you were before, or in this case, SIN! *"It's a fearful thing to fall into the hands of the living God."* [28] Notice verse thirty-nine continues, '*but believes* <u>TO THE SAVING OF THE SOUL</u>.' Our soul is being saved. **IF WE CONTINUE TO SIN DAILY AND THERE IS NOTHING WE CAN DO ABOUT IT THEN WE ARE SLAVES TO SIN; WE ARE NOT SAVED AS THE BIBLE TEACHES SALVATION. WE ARE STILL SLAVES TO SIN AND CHILDREN OF THE DEVIL.**

A couple of examples showing that we are not to continue in sin are what Jesus told those whom He had healed: the man at the Pool of Bethesda, in John 5:1-14. Jesus asked him if he wanted to be made well, and he replied *"I don't have anyone to put me into the water, etc..."* Jesus said to him, *"Rise, take up your bed and walk."* He did! In verse fourteen the man found Jesus in the temple and Jesus said to him, *"See, you have been made well.* **Sin no more, lest a worse thing come up on you**." The word 'well' means *to make whole*-body, soul and spirit. JESUS DID A COMPLETE WORK IN THE MAN; it was not just a physical healing. Not only was he healed of his disease, but he was forgiven and cleansed of sin!

Let's look at one more; here a woman was caught in adultery, and the scribes and Pharisees brought her to Jesus for judgment. Jesus knelt down and began to write on the ground, but they wouldn't let it go. Finally he told them, *"He who is without sin cast the first stone."* [29] Each one began to leave until they were all gone. When Jesus got up and saw only the woman, He asked where everyone was, has no one condemned you? *She said, "No one, Lord." He replied, "Neither do I condemn you;* **go and sin no more."** [30] Now, I ask you this question to ponder; Jesus told these people **to go and sin no more**, but if they couldn't help but sin every day, why would He have told them to go and sin no more? Why would He have told them to do something that was impossible? Jesus was not a liar, and that would have made Him a liar by implication.

What does Scripture say about continuing in sin? *"Whosoever commit-teth sin transgresseth also the law: for sin is the transgression of the law. And ye know that He was manifested to take away our sins; and in Him is no sin. Whosoever abideth in him sinneth not:* **whosoever sinneth** HATH NOT SEEN HIM, NEITHER KNOWN HIM. *Little children, let no man deceive you: he that doeth righteousness is righteous, even as He is righteous.* **He that committeth sin is of the devil; for the devil sinneth from the beginning.** *For this purpose* **the Son of God was manifested, that He might destroy the works of the devil.** *Whosoever is born of God* **doth not commit sin**; *for His seed remaineth in him: and he cannot sin, because he is born of God.* **In this the children of God are manifest, and the children of the devil: whosoever do**ETH **not righteousness is not of God, neither he that love**ETH **not his brother.** [31] I used the King James Version here because of the use of *'eth'* on the end of words. The *'eth'* means a continual process. Here we see that a person who continues to live in sin is not a Christian. Anytime a person has a life style of sin the Scripture says that person is of the devil.

This is what Scripture says about God and our relationship to Him; *"This then is the message which we have heard of Him, and declare unto you, that God is light, and in Him is* no darkness at all. *If we say that we have fellowship with Him, and* walk in darkness, we lie, *and do not the truth: But* **if we walk in the light, as He is in the light, we have fellowship one with another, and the blood of Jesus Christ his Son cleans**eth **us from all sin.** [32] In God **is no darkness at all!**" We cannot have fellowship with Him if we continue to walk in sin. Walk, according to Webster, means

Christianity

to pursue a course of action or way of life. Concerning sin John goes on to say: *"If we say that we have no sin, we deceive ourselves, and the truth is not in us. If we confess our sins, He is faithful and just to forgive us our sins, and to cleanse us from all unrighteousness. If we say that we have not sinned, we make Him a liar, and His word is not in us. My little children, these things write I unto you, **that ye sin not**. And if any man sin, we have an advocate with the Father, Jesus Christ the righteous: And He is the propitiation for our sins: and not for ours only, but also for the sins of the whole world."* [33] This is not talking about living under the sin principle or continual sin; it is speaking of the act of sin being an exception to the rule. What does all that mean? If you practice (you continually pursue a course of action or make it a way of life) sin, you are a slave of sin, but if you practice righteousness you are a slave to God. Does that mean we will never sin? No; it instead means that we don't make a habit of it. We are in a fallen world and we have an enemy, Satan; there is nothing he likes better than cause us to trip up, and he sets us up all the time for failure. But when we do sin, i.e. 'miss the mark', we know that we have an advocate, Jesus Christ, who is ever making intercession for us to God the Father so that, as 2 Timothy 2:25 says; *'if God perhaps will grant them repentance, so that they may know the truth, and that they may come to their senses and <u>escape the snare of the devil</u>, having been taken captive by him to do his will.'* In verse 19 of this chapter Paul says The Lord 'knoweth' them that are His. And, Let everyone that nameth the name of Christ <u>depart from iniquity</u>. This scripture is in reference to Galatians 6:1 *"Brethren, if a man is <u>overtaken</u> in any trespass, you who are spiritual <u>restore</u> such a one in a spirit of gentleness, considering yourself lest you also be tempted."* There are times when we, through **deception,** fall into the trap Satan has set for us and we are helpless to do anything. *'If we say that we have no sin, we **deceive** ourselves and the truth is not in us. If we confess our sins, He is faithful and just to forgive us our sins and to cleanse us from all unrighteousness.'* [34] If we CONFESS our **Sins**- Confess- admit we sinned, confess that sin to God the minute the Holy Spirit convicts us, confess what we did as sin (not a mistake) understanding it was against God and His holiness, and ask God to forgive us, with the determination that we, in submitting to God through the power of the Holy Spirit invested in us, will not continue to repeat the same offense. Who do we tell, and how do we confess? First we confess to God. I have sinned against You! If you are involved with others in the sin, confess to those you were involved with 'that you were in opposition to God; 'I have sinned against God in doing this thing.' If it has damaged the testimony of your church you are to go directly to the Pastor and or Elders of the church and confess your sin to them asking forgiveness. Notice God said, "*if we confess our sin He is FAITHFUL to forgive us our sin and CLEANSE us from ALL Unrighteousness.*" Confess our sin, i.e., what we did. That is not a blanket prayer when we pray – forgive us of our sin and cleanse us of our unrighteousness it is a deliberate naming of a particular sin we have committed when the Holy Spirit convicts us. Confession is directly related to not repeating the same offense; it is not just saying, like I've heard some of the younger generation say—'O, my bad!' and continue on in sin.

What 1 John 3 is talking about is a ***continual sinning without regard to God***, or flippantly saying without sincere disgust at your sin and truly being in anguish over our '*falling short of the glory of God*'[35] Saying something like, "Oh, forgive me Jesus, I didn't mean to do that!", using the excuse that I'm saved and nothing can take me out of His hand, or as I've heard; 'That's why we have it (referencing the doctrine 'once saved always saved') because I'm going to lie to not hurt some ones feelings.' That is a lie of convenience. A lie is a lie is a lie. "*But for the cowardly and unbelieving and abominable and murderers and immoral persons and sorcerers and idolaters **and all liars**, their part will be in the lake that burns with fire and brimstone, which is the second death.*" [36]

It is true nothing or no one can take you from God's hand. You can, however, by your blatant sin, disregarding His justness, holiness, and righteousness in an unrepentant state *fall from grace* as some say you cannot. Look at Galatians "*Stand fast therefore in the liberty by which Christ has made us free, and do not be entangled again with a yoke of bondage. Indeed I, Paul, say to you that if you become circumcised, Christ will profit you nothing. And I testify again to ever many who becomes circumcised that he is debtor to keep the whole law. You have become **estranged from Christ**, you to attempt to be justified by law; **you have fallen from grace**.*"
[37] Now I realize this is talking to Christians who were being encouraged to be circumcised i.e., live by the law, but the fact remains and the subject we are attending to here is whether or not it is possible to fall from grace. What is *estranged from Christ?* Webster defines *estranged* as to remove from customary environment or association, **to arouse enmity** or indifference in where there had formerly been love, affection or friendliness; ALIENATED, DISAFFECT; ESTRANGE implies the development of indifference or hostility with consequent separation or divorcement. DISAFFECT refers especially to those from whom loyalty is expected, and stresses the effects (as rebellion or discontent) of alienation without actual separation. Alienation of affection, development of hostility with the consequence of

Christianity

separation or divorcement! [38] What is being cut off the vine and thrown into the fire to be burned in John 15? Separation and divorcement!!

Let's look at another Scripture; this one is talking about turning from Christ back into sin in Hebrews, *'Therefore, leaving the discussion of the elementary principles of Christ, <u>let us go on to perfection</u>, not laying again the foundation of repentance from dead works and of faith toward God, of the doctrine of baptisms, of laying on of hands, of resurrection of the dead, and of eternal judgment. And this we will do if God permits. For it is **<u>impossible</u>** for those who were once enlightened, and have tasted the heavenly gift, and have become partakers of the Holy Spirit, and have tasted the good word of God and the powers of the age to come**, <u>if they fall away</u> to renew them again to repentance**, since they crucify again for themselves the Son of God, and put Him to an open shame. For the earth which drinks in rain that often comes upon it, and bears herbs useful for those by whom it is cultivated, receives blessing from God; but if it bears thorns and briars, is rejected and near to being cursed, **whose end is to be burned**."* [39] These are only two of the Scriptures referencing falling away from Salvation. For further study look at John 15:6, Hebrews 10:26-29, and 2 Peter 2:20-22.

I personally want to believe there are few <u>who are truly born again</u> that fall away, but that is my personal desire. I am not the judge or the one who will bring those before the judge. I know there are many people who have received Christ and have received false teaching, or have never been discipled, who are yet in the state where the foundation principles of the gospel have not been taught them, and they are walking in ignorance of the truth. I know many ministers of the gospel have relied on the Professors of the Seminaries they attended to teach them the truth, or have read life stories and doctrinal beliefs of many past 'great' men of God, and have not gotten in the Word and received instruction from the Holy Spirit without bias. Many have been taught from childhood certain doctrines and can only see Scripture through the lens of that doctrine, thereby being deceived and deceiving many. **Be warned!** Receiving false teaching is no excuse; many people willfully do not study the Scriptures and go by what they have been told by a preacher or another person whom they feel is 'knowledge-able' in the Word of God. They are depending on someone else to 'spoon feed' them into eternity. They don't want to grow up for themselves. TAKE HEED, YOU ARE RESPONSIBLE FOR YOUR OWN SALVATION. Philippians 2:12 says, '....**<u>work out your OWN salvation</u> with fear and trembling;**' Once you have heard the Gospel and received Jesus Christ as your Savior, it is your responsibility to know the truth, you have been given the Holy Spirit and

He is your teacher. *"Howbeit when he, the Spirit of truth, is come,* **He will guide you into all truth***: for He shall not speak of himself; but whatsoever He shall hear, that shall He speak: and* **He will shew you things to come***. He shall glorify me: for He shall receive of mine, and* **shall shew it unto you***. All things that the Father hath are mine: therefore said I, that He shall take of mine, and* shall shew it unto you*.*" [40] We have an abundance of Bibles in the United States and abundant Scriptural Teaching. If the Spirit of Christ is within you, then you will have the desire to study and search the Word for your life in the Spirit. When you stand before the throne of God Almighty, He is not going to ask you what church you went to, or who your preacher was, or who told you about Jesus. He is going to judge you by whether or not you, first of all believed (trusted) and **received** Him and His Word, second, whether or not you applied yourself to know His Word and third, whether or not you obeyed His Word. You can't stand on what your mother or father or anyone else knew or did. It will be you and God. Jesus says when relating the parable of the ten virgins who were waiting for the Bridegroom, there were five foolish virgins and five wise virgins, the five foolish virgins did not prepare for the Bridegroom's coming at a later time than they expected. While they were away purchasing more oil, the Bridegroom came, and those who were prepared went into the wedding with Him and the door was shut. Later the other virgins came and requested the door be opened. Verse twelve says, *"But he answered and said, 'Assuredly, I say to you,* ***I do not know you****.'* [41] Note two things; first: they were all virgins (representing Christians, or the church), second: He said, '*I don't know you*.' He didn't say 'You don't know me,' He said, "*I don't know you*." I tell you now; the time will come when you wish not only that you truly knew Him, but that He knew you. Don't squander your time on earthly things; get ready to meet Him. Know His Word. Like the Psalmist said, *"Thy word have I hid in my heart that I might not sin against You."* [42] That is another Scripture stating not only how, but that we are not helpless to sin against God. Get His Word in your heart. If you have been taught wrong doctrine or have neglected the Word of God in your life up to this point and are under conviction right now, it's not too late. You can confess your sin; confess your lack of getting into His Word and searching for the truth for yourself. Confess that you have relied on others to teach you the truth and walked in error because of it. Confess whatever the Holy Spirit brings to your mind that you have failed to do properly. Then begin to get into the Word of God and search diligently for the truth. Ask the Holy Spirit to guide you and teach you the truth.

Christianity

Let us look again at what the Scripture says about those who **HAVE RECEIVED** Christ as their Savior and <u>WALK IN THE TRUTH FOR A WHILE AND TURN BACK TO THE WORLD</u> and begin living as if Christ had not redeemed them from the sin principle. *"For it is **impossible** for those who were once enlightened, and have tasted the heavenly gift, and have become partakers of the good word of God and the powers of the age to come **if they fall away**, to renew them again unto repentance, since they crucify again for themselves the Son of God, and put Him to an open shame."* [43] Note here they were not snatched out of His hand *they fell away*! *"Every branch in Me **that does not bear fruit He takes away**; and every branch that bears fruit He prunes, that it may bear more fruit.* Here **God takes away those who do not bear fruit**! [44] Note that this is the same term, 'takes away', that was used by John the Baptist, *"Behold the Lamb of God who <u>takes away</u> the sin of the world."* [45]

Look back at the word repentance. Repent-to think differently afterwards, to reconsider and remorse from guilt, <u>INCLUDING REFORMATION</u>, or reversal of decisions. In other words it means to feel guilty to the point of changing your mind about who you are and what you do **TO THE POINT OF REFORMATION** *i.e.* change, or as *Webster* put it, **A REMOVAL** OR CORRECTION OF AN ABUSE, a wrong or error (in other words SIN). *"Most assuredly, I say to you, he who believes in Me, the works **that I do** **HE WILL DO** ALSO: and greater works than these he will do because I go to My Father.* [46] **He who has My commandments and <u>keeps them, it is he who loves Me</u>**. *And he who loves Me will be loved by My Father, and I will love him and manifest Myself to him.* [47] **He who does not love Me does not keep My words;..."** [48] *As God has said: "I will dwell in them and walk among them. I will be their God, and they shall be My people." Therefore, <u>Come out from among them and be separate</u>, says the Lord. **Do not touch what is unclean, and I will receive you**. I will be a Father to you, and you shall be My sons and daughters, says the Lord Almighty." "<u>Therefore, having these promises, beloved, **let us cleanse ourselves form all filthiness of the flesh and spirit, perfecting holiness** in the fear of God</u>."* [49] *"and Adam was not deceived, but the woman being deceived, fell into transgression. Nevertheless she will be saved in childbearing **if they continue in faith, love and holiness, with self-control**."* [50] *"This is a faithful saying, and these things I want you to affirm constantly, that* **those who have believed in God should be careful to maintain good works**. *These things are good and profitable to men. But avoid foolish disputes, genealogies, contentions, and strivings about the law; for they are unprofitable and useless. <u>Reject a divisive man after the first and second admonition</u>,* (I will interject here denominations are divisive) *knowing that <u>such a person is warped and sinning</u>, **being self condemned**.*" [51] "*Therefore <u>we must give the more earnest heed to the things we have heard</u> <u>lest we drift away</u>. For if the word spoken through angels proved steadfast and every transgression and disobedience received a just reward **how shall we escape if we neglect so great a salvation**.*" [52] "*For we have become partakers of Christ <u>if we hold the beginning of our confidence steadfast to the end</u>.*" [53] '*And He (Christ) said to me, "Do not seal the words of the prophecy of this book, for the time is at hand, He who is unjust, let him be unjust still; he who is filthy, let him be filthy still; he who is righteous, let him be righteous still; he who is holy, let him be holy still." "Behold, I am coming quickly and My reward is with Me, to give to everyone according to his work."*' [54]

Philip Yancy, in one of the 'OUR DAILY BREAD' devotionals makes this statement:

"God's terrible insistence on human freedom is so absolute that ***He granted us the power to live as though He does not exist***." Note what he says; "God has <u>granted us the power</u> to live as though He does not exist!" That's the power we have been given, the power to deny God's existence. We deny God's existence by doing the following: To live any old way we want. To spit in His face, curse Him, yes; He even gave man the authority to kill Him when He was in the flesh. To say we are Christians and yet by the lifestyle we live deny His authority and existence in our lives. To live after the flesh, fulfill its desires and not seek His face, His will and His purpose. Yes we have been granted the power to deny, deny, deny, the power over sin! We have dragged Jesus' blood through the streets with our denial of God's '<u>right</u>' to our lives. We say we are Christians but live as if "It's all about me." Many people are living to fulfill their desires. After all, that's what walking after the flesh is all about: **ME**. It's my way or the highway! I did it my way! That my friend is the ultimate LOVE of God; He made us, He is our very breath, without His supply of the perfect blend of elements in the air we could not even breathe, yet He *granted* us the *power* to live as though He does not exist! How awesome of a God is that! O What love! God gave His only Son that we ***may not*** perish! He has given His best gift so that we may come to Him, fellowship with Him, love, adore, and follow in His steps. And yet we treat Him as if He doesn't exist almost daily. Remember the word 'let' in the story of creation. God gave Adam the power and the choice to subdue the earth. Although he had the power he chose not to subdue it. We have been given the power of the Holy Spirit to become the children of God and to subdue sin in our lives. '*Therefore <u>**do not LET sin reign**</u> in your mortal body so that you obey its lusts, and do not* *go on presenting the members of your body to sin as instruments of unrighteousness; but present yourselves to God as those alive from the dead, and your members as instruments of righteousness to God.'* [55] God told Israel, *"You have forgotten Me days without number!"* [56] How that broke the heart of a loving, merciful God, to set them apart as a special treasure and then for them to forget Him! Are we any different today? Yet we've been given the Holy Spirit, the very Spirit of Christ <u>within</u> us, to guide, teach, comfort and to conform us into the image of God. And then we have the audacity to say and walk like were still bound to the old sin nature!

Read Ezekiel 18; I'll quote verses 21-24. *"Moreover, if the wicked one repents of all the sins that he committed and keeps all My laws and does what is just and right, he shall live; he shall not die. None of the transgressions he committed shall be remembered against him; because of the righteousness he has practiced, he shall live. Is it my desire that a wicked person shall die? –says the Lord God. It is rather that he shall turn back from his ways and live. So too, if a righteous person turns away from his righteousness and does wrong, practicing the very abominations that the wicked person practiced, shall he live?* **None of the righteous deeds that he did shall be remembered; because of the treachery he has practiced and the sins he has committed—because of these, he shall die."**

What can I say? Only to repeat the words of Paul to the Corinthians and Hebrews:
"But I am fear, lest by any means as the serpent beguiled Eve through his subtility, so your **minds should be corrupted from the simplicity that is in Christ.** [57] **For if the message spoken by angels was binding, and every violation and disobedience received its just punishment, <u>how shall we escape</u> if we ignore such a great salvation?** *This salvation, which was first announced by the Lord, was confirmed to us by those who heard him."* [58] Make no mistake God is an awesome and Holy God and those that worship Him must worship Him in spirit and truth. He says in Leviticus *"By those who come near Me I must be regarded as Holy; and before all the people I must be glorified."* [59] *"What agreement can there be between temple of God and idols? For we are the temple of the living God; even as God said,* <u>I will dwell in</u> *and with and among them and* <u>will walk in</u> *and with and among them, and I will be their God, and they shall be My people."* [60] Notice He, God, says, *"I will dwell in them."* If God is in us how can we continue to sin? We cannot! That is the meaning of 1 John 3:9, *'No one who is born of God practices sin,* **<u>because His seed abides in</u>**

Eternal Security

*him; and **he cannot sin**, because he is born of God.'* I know this is hard to understand because we have been taught otherwise. I am afraid that in our struggle to explain our continuance in sin after we have 'accepted' Christ, we have misconstrued the Word of God. Salvation is a Work of God in our inner man. I am concerned that in our zealousness for new converts we have not preached, as Jesus did, the necessity of counting the cost.[61] Peter says, *"For if after they have escaped the pollutions of the world through the knowledge of the Lord and Savior Jesus Christ, they are again entangled therein, and overcome, the latter end is worse with them than the beginning. For it had been better for them not to have know the way of righteousness, than, after they have know it, to turn from the holy commandment delivered unto them."*[62] Christianity in the United States has been the 'norm' into this decade; that popularity is waning due to the lack of true Christians and the exercise of the power Salvation has to change lives. We have doctrines to explain the lack of power in our lives and in essence denied the Holy Spirit's place and authority in our lives, and in doing so, there are thousands, if not millions, of people living with the false security of salvation and thousands, if not millions, who reject the only hope of salvation available to them. That is the reason Paul says in Corinthians, '*So, come out from among them [unbelievers], and separate (sever) yourselves from them, says the Lord, and touch not [any] unclean thing; **then** I will receive you kindly and treat you with favor,* [1a] *And I will be a Father to you, and you shall be My sons and daughters, says the Lord Almighty.*[1b] *THEREFORE, SINCE these [great] promises are ours, beloved, **let us cleanse ourselves from everything that contaminates and defiles body and spirit**, and bring [our] consecration to completeness in the [reverential] fear of God."* [63] I would like to reiterate here that our soul is being saved; we have been taught many things that are contrary to the Word of God. As we grew up we learned to react or respond to different situations in all sorts of ways. Our 'soul' i.e. conscience (brain–computer) was programmed to believe and act certain ways according to what was going on in our lives. That is the reason Paul tells us in Romans 12:1-2 that we are to '*present our bodies as a living sacrifice to God which is our reasonable service and do not be conformed to this world but be transformed by the renewing of our mind.*" I want to look at three words in this Scripture. Present, conformed and transformed. **Present** according to Webster's means to make a gift, to give or bestow formally, [64] and according to Strong's comes from two root words meaning to stand beside, to exhibit, substantiate or bring before or yield. [65] In other words, we are to offer our bodies or yield to God as a living sacrifice, exhibiting,

117

confirming and embodying His nature. We do this by **not** *conforming (to this world)*, *i.e.*, to be similar or identical, or to be obedient or compliant, to adapt oneself to prevailing standards or customs.[66] But rather we are to be *trans-formed*-to change character or condition, to convert [67] (the original Greek meaning) metamorphoo – change, fashioned, transformed. [68] How? By the renewing of our mind! Ephesians 5:26 says, *"That He might sanctify and cleanse her with the washing of the water of the word."* As we get into the Word of God, study and meditate on it, our minds are cleansed and sanctified (set apart for a sacred purpose-Webster). King David said in Psalm 119:11, *"Thy word have I hid in my heart that I might not sin against You."*

The reason I have been able to write this book is because I have hidden the Word of God in my heart. As I have written the Holy Spirit would bring up the Word or Scripture to make each point. There are many times I have had to pick up my Bible and look up a Scripture so as not to misquote or find the exact Scriptural address. I have diligently studied the Bible because I was hungry for the truth. There was a time that I studied it because I did not understand Salvation and I thought I had to obey every word in order to be saved, but that was out of fear of going to hell, not because of love. I learned through studying the Bible what true Salvation is, what it means to be Born Again, what Baptism is, and that there is more than one Baptism, the Baptism of Repentance-Water and the Baptism of the Holy Spirit where the Spirit is imparted to me as a believer to teach me, guide me, convict me, etc. I have learned that *I* cannot live the Word. I have to yield to the Holy Spirit and allow Him to walk it out in me. The following chapters contain the Scriptures I was taught by The Holy Spirit to help me get the Word into my heart. When He gave them to me I typed them out –back then on a typewriter and began reading them aloud every day, mostly in confession to my Father (God) in prayer. Talk about transforming your mind! That will do it. There are times the enemy will come in like a flood and jerk the spiritual rug from under you, and he has done so to me many times, I have found myself as it were in the 'mire' wondering what happened. The Spirit always draws me back and reminds me of the Word. I repent grievously and God is always faithful. It is the faithfulness of Christ that saves us. As we trust in His finished work He renews us. The reason for the title of this book, *Christianity: A Death and A Resurrection* is because that is what it is. I identify with Jesus Christ on the cross, I died with Him, and was buried in the waters of Baptism, I was resurrected to new life in Him and as I abide (live my life) in Him I am changed into the image of God in Christ.[69]

CHAPTER THIRTEEN

[1] Matthew 18:16
[2] John 1:29
[3] Romans 1:16
[4] Romans 10:8-9 [4]
[5] Romans 10:13 [4]
[6] John 10:28 [4]
[7] Romans 10:10
[8] Page 974 [7]
[9] Page 741 [6]
[10] #1941 [6]
[11] 2 Corinthians 5:21
[12] Colossians 1·13 [4]
[13] Page 940 [7]
[14] 2 Corinthians 5: 17
[15] Romans 8:13 [4]
[16] Romans 11:22 [4]
[17] John 15:2, 6
[18] Isaiah 59:2
[19] #726 'pluck' from #138 [6]
[20] James 1:12
[21] James 1:12-15
[22] John 1:12
[23] Ephesians 2:1 [8]
[24] Colossians 2:13-15 [4]
[25] Page 626 [7]
[26] # 684 [6]
[27] http://www.wordsmyth.net/draw
[28] Hebrews 10:31
[29] John 8:1-7
[30] John 8: 11
[31] 1 John 3:4-10
[32] 1 John 1: 5-7
[33] 1 John 1: 8-10 & 1 John 2: 1-2
[34] 1 John 1:8–9
[35] Romans 3:23
[36] Revelation 21:8
[37] Galatians 5:1-4

[38] Webster's, page 285[7]
[39] Hebrews 6: 1-8
[40] John 16:13-15
[41] Matthew 25: 1-12
[42] Psalms 119:11
[43] Hebrews 6:4-6
[44] John 15:2
[45] John 1:29
[46] John 14:12
[47] John 14:21
[48] John 14:24
[49] 2 Corinthians 6:16b-7:1
[50] 1Timothy 2:14-15
[51] Titus 3:8-11
[52] Hebrews 2:1-3a
[53] Hebrews 3:14
[54] Revelations 22:10-12
[55] Romans 6: 12-13
[56] Jeremiah 2:32
[57] 2 Corinthians 11:3 (Gen. 3:4)
[58] Hebrews 2:2-3
[59] Leviticus 10:3, 12
[60] 2 Corinthians 6:16
[61] Luke 14:28
[62] 2 Peter 2:20-21
[63] 2 Corinthians 6:17-7:1 (Ex. 25:8; 29:45; Lev. 26:12; Jer. 31:1; Ezek. 37:27)
[64] Page 672, *verb, definition 2, 3*[7]
[65] #3936[6]
[66] Page 175[7]
[67] Page 940[7]
[68] #3339[6]
[69] Galatians 2:20

Chapter Fourteen

Who WE ARE in Christ

In the New Living Translation, John states, *'Jesus spoke to the people once more and said, "I am the light of the world. **If you follow me, you won't have to walk in darkness**, because you will have the light that leads to life."*[1] The New American Standard says it this way; *'Then Jesus again spoke to them, saying, "I am the Light of the world; he who follows Me **will not** walk in the darkness, but will have the Light of life."'* So here we see; we *WILL NOT* WALK —practice, or continually act out—in darkness-sin. Remember in Genesis where God, talking to Cain, had told him that *"Sin is crouching at the door, eager to control you. But **you must subdue it and be its master**."*[2] Didn't God say the same thing to Adam and Eve in the beginning, SUBDUE the earth? And notice too that this was after the fall! God insinuated that Cain could subdue sin! If Cain, being without the Holy Spirit, could have subdued sin, why is it that Christians filled with the Spirit cannot? Here is where I believe the definition of 'let' comes into play in the lives most Christians. We have a <u>LACK OF POWER OF EFFECTIVE AUTHORITY THROUGH INADVERTENCE OR NEGLIGENCE OF THE WORD</u> and/or the will of God **or simply because we do not believe it**.

As believers of Jesus Christ, we have been given the Holy Spirit to live within us. He has given us the power to become the children of God. Jesus praying for the believers says; *"I do not pray for these alone, but also for those who will believe in Me through their word; that they all may be one, as You, Father, are in Me, and I in You; that they may be one in Us, that the world may believe that You sent Me. And **the glory which You gave Me I have given them**, that they may be one just as We are one; I in them and You in Me; **that they may be made perfect in one**."*[3] And, *"The* *highest heavens belong to the LORD, **but the earth He has given to man.**"* [4]*"For assuredly, I say to you, <u>whoever says</u> to this mountain, 'Be removed and be cast into the sea, <u>and **does not doubt** in his heart</u>, **but believes that those things which he says** will be done, <u>he will have whatever he says</u>. Therefore I say to you, <u>whatever things you ask when you pray, believe that you receive them, and you will have them</u>."* [5] In writing to the various churches of his day, Paul addresses the people of the congregations as '*the church (assembly) of God which is in Corinth, to those **consecrated and purified and made holy** in Christ Jesus, [who are] selected and called to be saints'*,'[6] in Ephesus, *to the saints (the consecrated, set-apart ones) at Ephesus who are also faithful and loyal and steadfast in Christ Jesus.* [7] in Philippi, '*to all the saints (God's consecrated people) in Christ Jesus who are at Philippi,'* [8] to the Colossians, '***To the saints (the consecrated people of God) and believing and faithful brethren in Christ.*** [9] In Jude we find Jude addressing the church in the same fashion: '*to those who are called, **dearly loved by God the Father** and separated (set apart) and kept for Jesus Christ.*' [10] And lastly, we are given the armor of God. [11]

I have shared below a means through which we can use the Scriptural promises contained in the Word as a means of putting on the full armor of God. This is by no means the only way or the only Scriptures that can be used; these are just the ones I have used. There are times when I may change the order or delete or add certain Scriptures. As we read and quote aloud daily the Scriptures we not only hide the Word in our hearts, but we build our faith (trust) in Him and His Word. I have put these Scriptures in the first person fully identifying by faith in each promise. I cannot express how important it is to not only continually quote, but to meditate upon these and many of the Scriptures previously used in this book so as to keep them in forefront of our minds about who we are and what we have been given in Christ Jesus. The enemy is in a full scale war against our souls and the moment we let down our defenses by not taking up the full armor of God he comes in like a flood and has us in derision. The Word of God *is* a two edged sword [12] and it is our only offensive weapon against the enemy. All the other armor is defensive in nature and must be taken up constantly to keep the enemy from penetrating and gaining a foothold in our lives as Christians. The Shield of Faith (trust) is the most important defensive weapon. Without Faith it is IMPOSSIBLE to please God and one will not receive anything from Him. [13] Please understand this: faith is TRUST, total reliance upon God to do what we cannot do. It is not only believing God can, but that **He already has**! I have titled it Our Identity in Christ.

Our Identity in Christ

In Light of Armor of God

YOU, O GOD said, "I WILL DWELL IN THEM AND WALK AMONG THEM; AND I WILL BE THEIR GOD, AND THEY SHALL BE MY PEOPLE. Therefore, [I have] COME OUT FROM THEIR MIDST AND BE [come] SEPARATE. AND [I] DO NOT TOUCH WHAT IS UNCLEAN; [So that You] will welcome [me]. And You will be a Father to me, and I shall be a daughter to You, [14] *I will worship toward Your Holy temple, and praise Your Name for Your loving-kindness and Your truth; for You have magnified Your Word above all Your Name. In the day when I cried out, You answered me, and made me BOLD with strength in my soul. Though I walk in the midst of trouble, You will revive me; You will stretch out Your hand against the wrath of my enemies, and Your right hand will save me. You will perfect that which concerns me; Your mercy, O Lord, endures forever; do not forsake the works of Your hands.* [15] *Forever, O Lord, Your Word is settled in heaven. Your faithfulness endures to all generations.* [16] *Jesus is LORD over my spirit, soul and body.*

BELT OF TRUTH
I have been called by You, O Lord to be Your own holy child. You made me holy by means of Christ Jesus just as You did for all people everywhere who call upon the name of our Lord Jesus Christ, their Lord and ours. [17] *But as it is, I desire a better country, that is, a heavenly one. Therefore You O' God are not ashamed to be called my God; for You have prepared a city for me.* [18] *YOU SAID WHATEVER THINGS I DESIRE WHEN I PRAY, IF I BELIEVE THAT I RECEIVE THEM, I SHALL HAVE THEM.* [19] *And this is the confidence I have in You, IF I ASK ANYTHING <u>according to Your will</u>, You hear me, and IF I KNOW YOU HEAR ME, WHATEVER I ASK, I KNOW THAT I WILL HAVE WHAT I ASKED.* [20] *Jesus, You, came that I might have life and have it more abundantly.* [21]

BREAST PLATE OF RIGHTEOUSNESS
I am a new creation; old things have passed away, all things are new. Now all things are of God for I have been reconciled to Him through Jesus Christ, He has given to me the ministry of reconciliation and has committed me to the Word of reconciliation. I am an ambassador for Christ, God pleading through me for others to be reconciled to God, for God made Christ, who knew no sin to be sin for me that I might become the

righteousness of God in Christ. [22] *neither will I say, lo here! Or lo there! For behold the kingdom of God is within me!* [23] Therefore I hold the thoughts, feelings, and purposes of His heart. *The love of God has been shed abroad in my heart by the Holy Spirit; Your love abides in me richly.* [24] *God is love. I live in love and live in God and God in me.* [25] *I know that no one who is born of God sins; but He who was born of God keeps me, and the evil one does not touch me.* [26]

GOSPEL OF PEACE
I fear not, for God has not given me a spirit of fear but of power, of love, and a sound mind. [27] *God is on my side.* [28] *I will not be afraid of ten thousands of people who have set themselves against me round about. He has left His peace with me, His peace He has given to me; not as the world gives, does He give to me.* [29] *I will not let my heart be troubled; neither will I let it be afraid. Though I may be troubled on every side, yet I will not be distressed; I may be perplexed, but not forsaken, cast down, but not destroyed; always bearing about in the body the dying of the Lord Jesus, that the life of Jesus might be manifest in my body.* [30] *For which cause I also suffer these things; nevertheless I am not ashamed; for I know Whom I have believed, and am persuaded that YOU ARE ABLE TO KEEP that which I HAVE COMMITTED unto You against that day.* [31] *Your, Peace You left with me; Your peace You have given to me; not as the world gives did You give to me. Therefore, I will not let my heart be troubled, nor will let it be fearful.* [32] *I am born of God therefore I have overcome the world, and this is my victory that overcomes the world, MY FAITH."* [33] I am a world over comer because I'm born of God. I represent the Father and Jesus well. I am a useful member in the Body of Christ *'for I am Your workmanship, created in Christ Jesus for good works, which You have prepared beforehand so that I would walk in them."* [34] *My Father, You are all the while EFFECTUALLY* AT WORK IN ME, BOTH TO WILL AND TO DO YOUR GOOD PLEASURE.* [35] *Who shall separate me from Your love, Christ? Shall tribulation, or distress, or persecution, or famine, or nakedness, or peril, or sword? Nay in ALL these things I AM MORE THAN A CONQUEROR because YOU love me.* [36] *As I wait upon YOU, YHWH, You renew my strength; I mount up with wings as eagles; I run and do not become weary, and I walk and do not faint.* [37]

*Producing or able to produce a desired effect: ADEQUATE, EFFECT -To bring about/something produced by an agent REALITY-FACT

SHIELD OF FAITH
I am delivered from this present evil world because You, Jesus gave Your life for my sins.[38] *I am seated with, You (Christ) in heavenly places.*[39] *For You, O Lord, have rescued me from the domain of darkness, and transferred me to the kingdom of Your beloved Son.*[40] *The law of the Spirit of Life in Christ Jesus has made me free from the law of sin and death.*[41] *You, O Lord are my light and my salvation; whom shall I fear? You, O Lord are the strength of my life; of whom shall I be afraid?*[42] *I am of God and as Your child I have overcome the world, for You are Greater in me than he who is in the world.*[43] *I tread upon serpents and scorpions and over all the power of the enemy.*[44] *Jesus, You came that I may have life, and I have it abundantly.*[45] *I take up the shield of faith with which I am able to extinguish all the flaming arrows of the evil one.*[46] *I do not walk in condemnation because I am in Christ Jesus, and because I do not walk after the flesh but after the Spirit. I am a believer and not a doubter.*[47] *Since Jesus the Son of God is my High Priest and has gone up into the heavens; I hold fast my confession of faith,*[48] *Without faith I cannot please Him, so I come to You, O God and I believe that You are and that You reward me because I seek You*[49] I decide to walk by faith and practice faith. *My faith comes by hearing and hearing by the Word of God.*[50] *Jesus, You are the author and finisher of my faith.*[51] *Because I have departed out from the world, I desire to touch nothing unclean; I have come out of the midst of the world, to purify myself, to You, O LORD.*[52] *You, O LORD will go before me, and You (God of Israel) will be my rear guard.*[53] You've got my back!!!

HELMET OF SALVATION
I have the mind of Christ.[54] *Because I abide in You and Your Word abides in me, I can say what I will and it shall be done unto me.*[55] *I let the Word dwell in me richly. You who have begun a good work in me will continue it until the day of Christ.*[56] *You will keep me in perfect peace because my mind is stayed upon You, O Lord.*[57] *O, LORD, I cry unto You; come quickly to me. Hear my voice when I cry unto You. Let my prayer be set before You as incense and the lifting up of my hands as the evening sacrifice. Set a watch, over my mouth; keep the door of my lips. Let not my heart be drawn to any evil thing, to practice wicked works with men that work iniquity: and do not let me eat of their delicacies.*[58] *Jesus, You have been made unto me wisdom, righteousness, sanctification, and redemption.*[59] *I can do all things through You, Christ who strengthens me.*[60] *I am redeemed from the curse of the law, because You, Jesus bore my sickness and carried my diseases in Your own body.*[61] *You bore my sins in Your body on*

the cross, so that I might DIE TO SIN AND LIVE TO RIGHTEOUSNESS; for by Your wounds I was healed.[62] Therefore; *whatever I bind (forbid) on earth shall have been bound (forbidden) in heaven; and whatever I loose (permit) on earth shall have been loosed (permitted) in heaven.*[63]

THE SWORD OF THE SPIRIT
For Your Word O, God is living and active and sharper than any two-edged sword, and piercing as far as the division of soul and spirit, of both joints and marrow, and able to judge the thoughts and intents of my heart. [64] *I have turned away from the vain things of the world to You, living God.* [65] *I have proclaimed glad tidings of righteousness in the great assembly [tidings of uprightness and right standing with God. Behold, I have not restrained my lips, as You know, O Lord. I have not concealed Your righteousness within my heart; I have proclaimed Your faithfulness and Your salvation. I have not hid away Your steadfast love and Your truth from the great assembly.* [66] *I have believed and have been baptized am being saved. These signs accompany me because I have believed: in Jesus name I cast out demons, I speak with new tongues; I will pick up serpents, and if I drink any deadly poison, it will not hurt me; I lay hands on the sick, and they recover.* [67] *I am a chosen generation, a royal priesthood, a holy nation. Your own special person, I proclaim Your praises You have called me out of darkness into Your marvelous light.* [68]

If you will continually quote the Word, it builds your faith (trust); just doing this for a while and quitting before you have it down in your heart and spirit will not work. The enemy will come in and still the Word if you give him place. I have learned this from personal experience. The Word only works by trust, doubt will get you nowhere. Quote it until you believe it in your heart. That is the only way it works.

For more see Appendix 3 & 4

Just a word concerning the Words of our Mouth: Remember in Hebrews it says, "*The word of God is alive and powerful......*" [69] In the book of James it talks about how we control a ship with a small rudder and a horse with a small bit in its mouth. "*So also the tongue is a small part of the body, and yet it boasts of great things. Behold how great a forest is set aflame by such a small fire! And the tongue is a fire, the very world of iniquity; the tongue is set among our members as that which defiles the entire body, and sets on fire the course of our life, and is set on fire by hell.*" [70] Proverbs says, "*Death and life are in the power of the tongue,*" [71] We can say all day long that we believe something but what we constantly *confess* will determine whether or not we truly believe it in our heart. *"But whatever comes out of the mouth comes from the heart,"* [72] It's your <u>continual talk</u> that proves what you really believe in your heart. For example, when I get up one morning and my head hurts the first thing I say is, "I have a headache." I call my friends and ask them to pray for me. We agree in prayer that Jesus died for my sin and by His stripes I am healed. Even so, the ache persists. To each person I come in contact with that day, I say, "I don't feel too well, I have a headache." I have just confessed what I really believe. The pain is more real than the healing. Think back to the word faith TRUST; remember it's the substance or the ultimate reality of change and manifestation.

CHAPTER FOURTEEN

[1] John 8:12
[2] Genesis 4:7[2]
[3] John 17:20-23 [8]
[4] Psalm 115:16[5]
[5] Mark 11:23-24[8]
[6] 1 Corinthians 1:2[1]
[7] Ephesians 1:1[1]
[8] Philippians 1:1[1]
[9] Colossians 1:2[1]
[10] Jude 1[1]
[11] Ephesians 6:13-18
[12] Hebrews 4:12
[13] Hebrews 11:6
[14] 2 Corinthians 6:16-7:1
[15] Psalm 138:2, 3 & 7
[16] Psalm 119:89, 90
[17] 1 Corinthians 1:2
[18] Hebrews 11:16
[19] Mark 11:4
[20] 1 John 5:14, 15
[21] John 10:10
[22] 2 Corinthians 5:17-21
[23] Luke 17:21
[24] Romans 5:5
[25] 1 John 4:16
[26] 1 John 5:18
[27] 2 Timothy 1:7
[28] Romans 8:31
[29] Psalm 3:6
[30] 2 Corinthians 4:8, 9
[31] 2 Timothy 1:12
[32] John 14:27
[33] 1 John 5:4
[34] Ephesians 2:10
[35] Philippians 2:13
[36] Romans 8:35, 37
[37] Isaiah 40:31
[38] Galatians 1:4

Who WE ARE in Christ

[39] Ephesians 2:6
[40] Colossians 1:13
[41] Romans 8:2
[42] Psalm 27:1
[43] 1 John 4:4
[44] Luke 10:19
[45] John 10:10
[46] Ephesians 6:16
[47] Romans 8:1
[48] Hebrews 4:14
[49] Hebrews 11:6
[50] Romans 10:17
[51] Hebrews 12:2
[52] 2 Corinthians 6:18
[53] Isaiah 52:11 & 12
[54] 1 Corinthians 2:16
[55] John 15:7
[56] Colossians 3:16
[57] John 14:27, Isaiah 26:3
[58] Psalm 141:1-4
[59] 1 Corinthians 1:30
[60] Philippians 4:13
[61] Galatians 3:13 & Matthew 8:17
[62] 1 Peter 2:24
[63] Matthew 18:18
[64] Hebrews 4:12
[65] Acts 14:15
[66] Psalm 40:10
[67] Mark 16:16-18
[68] 1Peter 2:9
[69] Hebrews 4:12
[70] James 3: 3-6[4]
[71] Proverbs 18:21[8]
[72] Matthew 15:18

Chapter Fifteen

The Power and/or Authority In Us

The gifts of the Spirit were not only for the New Testament Church. As the church of God today we are weak, helpless and destitute. I have pondered, prayed, and sought God on why this is. I haven't seen the power I have been talking about in my own life much less the majority of the 'church.' For example, somehow we have decided we can VOTE righteousness into our culture. The Lord recently showed me through the Word that we don't tarry or wait before the HIM. *"And behold, I will send forth upon you what My Father has promised; but remain in the city [Jerusalem]* <u>*until* you are clothed with power from on high*</u>*."* [1] Remember the definition of unto: until +to, i.e. remain unto the clothing of power from on high. *This is where we, myself included, have failed; we have not waited, remained i.e., tarried before the Lord long enough to be clothed with power from on high.* In the previous chapter under the 'Gospel of Peace' I quoted the Scripture, *"They that wait upon the Lord ..."* or as I quote it; *"As I wait upon the Lord..."* Jesus said He would not leave us orphans,[2] yet the majority of the church exemplifies just that—we look like orphans. There is just as much sickness, disease or (dis-ease), spiritual warfare, and deception today as there was in the time of the New Testament. We, as believers have received portions of the Scripture as for us today but not all Scripture. We have received a partial Salvation message mostly because of ignorance but also because we don't believe we can walk in the power and authority of Christ Jesus. That is manipulation of the grossest sort where the lives of people are desperate for Salvation and deliverance. *"For the mystery of iniquity doth already work: only he who now letteth will let, until he be taken out of the way. And then shall that Wicked be revealed, whom the LORD shall consume with the spirit of His mouth, and shall destroy with the brightness of His coming; Even him, whose coming is after the working of Satan with all power and signs and lying wonders, and deceivableness of unrighteousness in that perish;* BECAUSE THEY RECEIVED NOT THE LOVE OF THE TRUTH, THAT THEY MIGHT BE SAVED. AND FOR THIS CAUSE GOD SHALL SEND THEM STRONG DELUSION, THAT THEY SHOULD BELIEVE A LIE: THAT THEY ALL MIGHT BE DAMNED WHO BELIEVED NOT THE TRUTH, BUT HAD PLEASURE IN UNRIGHTEOUSNESS."[3]

The following are some Scriptures that reflect the reality of the power of Christ in the life of a Christian.

- *When the crowds saw it, they were struck with fear and awe; and they recognized God and praised and thanked Him, Who had given such power and authority to men.*
- *Jesus answered, You would not have any power or authority whatsoever against (over) Me if it were not given you from above. For this reason the sin and guilt of the one who delivered Me over to you is greater.*
- *but you will receive power when the Holy Spirit has come upon you; and you shall be witnesses to Me in Jerusalem, and in all Judea and Samaria, and to the end of the earth.*
- *But when Peter saw this, he replied to the people, 'Men of Israel, why are you amazed at this, or why do you gaze at us, as if by our own power or piety we had made him walk?*
- *And we also [especially] thank God continually for this, that when you received the message of God [which you heard] from us, you welcomed it not as the word of [mere] men, but as it truly is, the Word of God, which is effectually at work in you who believe [exercising its superhuman power in those who adhere to and trust in and rely on it].*
- *For I am not ashamed of the gospel, for it is the power of God for salvation to everyone who believes, to the Jew first and also to the Greek.*
- *For the word of the cross is foolishness to those who are perishing, but to us who are being saved it is the power of God.*

Christianity

- *For since in the wisdom of God the world through its wisdom did not come to know God, God was well-pleased through the foolishness of the message preached <u>to save those who believe</u>.*
- *For indeed Jews ask for signs and Greeks search for wisdom; but we preach Christ crucified, to Jews a stumbling block and to Gentiles foolishness, but to those who are the called, both Jews and Greeks, <u>Christ the power of God</u> and the wisdom of God.*
- *<u>But we have this treasure in earthen vessels</u>, so that the surpassing greatness of <u>the power will be of God and not from ourselves.</u>*
- *And He has said to me, "My grace is sufficient for you, <u>for power is made perfect in weakness,</u> therefore, I will boast all the more gladly, about my weaknesses, <u>so that Christ's power may rest on me.</u>*
- *I pray that the eyes of your heart may be enlightened, so that you will know what is the hope of His calling, what are the riches of the glory of His inheritance in the saints, and what is <u>the surpassing greatness of His power toward us</u> who believe.*
- *For this reason also, since the day we heard of it, we have not ceased to pray for you and to ask that you may <u>be filled with the knowledge of His will in all spiritual wisdom and understanding</u>, so that you will walk in a manner worthy of the Lord, to <u>please Him in all respects, bearing fruit in every good work and increasing in the knowledge of God</u>; <u>strengthened with all power</u>, according to His glorious might, <u>for the attaining of all steadfastness and patience</u>; joyously giving thanks to the Father, who has <u>qualified us to share in the inheritance of the saints</u> in Light.*
- *<u>For God has</u> not <u>given us a spirit</u> of fear, but of <u>power</u> and of <u>love</u> and of a <u>sound mind</u> or <u>discipline</u>.*
- *Grace and peace be multiplied unto you in the knowledge of God, and of Jesus our Lord. According as <u>His divine power hath given unto us all things that pertain unto life and godliness,</u> through the knowledge of Him that hath called us to glory and virtue. Whereby are given unto us exceeding great and precious promises: that by these <u>ye might be partakers of the divine nature</u>, having escaped the corruption that is in the world through lust.*

What is the purpose of this power that God has chosen to transfuse us with? *That <u>the righteous requirement of the law might be fulfilled in us</u> who do not walk according to the flesh but according to the Spirit.* [19]

CHAPTER FIFTEEN

[1] Luke 24:49
[2] John 14:18
[3] 2 Thessalonians 2:7-11
[4] Matthew 9:8[1]
[5] John 19:11[1]
[6] Acts 1:8[8]
[7] Acts 3:12[4]
[8] 1 Thessalonians 2:13[1]
[9] Romans 1:16[4]
[10] 1 Corinthians 1:18[4]
[11] 1 Corinthians 1:21-24[4]
[12] 2 Corinthians 4:7[4]
[13] 2 Corinthians 12:9[5]
[14] Ephesians 1:18[4]
[15] Ephesians 1:19[4]
[16] Colossians 1:9 -12
[17] 2 Timothy 1:7
[18] 2 Peter 1:2-5
[19] Romans 8:4[8]

Chapter Sixteen

The Enemy and Warfare

The enemy will stop at nothing to keep God's Word from going forth! Immediately after writing the previous chapter, the enemy brought a full scale attack on my life. He came in from every direction, first through things at church, then through circumstances with my husband, problems with my children & grandchildren beyond my control, then physical attacks and finally exhaustion. Although I battled with the Word for a season as I have previously suggested, at the point of physical pain and exhaustion I began to crumble. I began to fall asleep while praying or reading the Word. I felt like the heavens were brass, I felt alone, and I had no one to stand with me (no one to pray for me or with me that I could express where I was at this point). I even got offended! Offense is a big tool of the enemy. In the midst of the offense he began to bring back remembrances of past failures and sin, old hurts and new ones. Jesus warned us that offense would come in Matthew 18:7. Then after almost two years I even began to question my salvation. That's where the devil wanted me: to question God and His Word! Remember his first question to Eve in the Garden, *"Hath God said?"* [1] But I kept praying; I know Your Word is true, I know Your Word. The enemy would whisper, "you're just praying vain repetitions, you're just saying those Scriptures but deep down inside you know that's not you." Before long I found myself just saying, "Father I know You are on the throne and in control of all things. I know Jesus is Lord, He is risen and seated at Your right hand. I know Your Word is true. I know that all things that You have decreed will come to pass." I kept reading my Bible although it felt like I wasn't getting anything out of it. Still the onslaught continued. Hoping what seemed like was against hope[2] one day, as I was reading the Bible praying, asking God to 'please speak to me, give me something to believe in,' when I read: *"In this you greatly rejoice, even though for a little while, <u>if necessary</u>,* **you have been distressed by various trials, <u>so that the proof of your faith</u>,** *being more precious than gold which is perishable, even though* **<u>tested by fire</u>, may be found to result in praise and glory and honor at the revelation of Jesus Christ;** *and though you have not seen Him, you love Him, and though you do not see Him now, but believe in Him, you greatly rejoice with joy inexpressible and full of glory...."*[3] Praise God, He showed me He had me the whole time; look back at the words italicized and underlined 'if necessary' as I am editing this section those words popped out at me. You see we don't really know ourselves, nor our heart, Jeremiah 17:9, says, *"Our hearts are deceitful above all things, desperately wicked.."* one translation says it *'is mortally sick'*, the Jewish Study Bible says , *"Most devious is the heart; it is perverse…"* I needed to know some things that were still in my heart. Although, I kept praying that I would be able to give Him the glory only He deserves by my life, I had to understand I didn't really know myself, there were things 'hidden' in my heart that had not been dealt with. I recently through His mercy came to understand more fully submission to authority-delegated authority. God is Sovereign. He has set delegated authority over all of us, and not one of us is exempt from being under authority. I've been reading over, and over, and listening to the 'Go Bible' through the Old and New Testaments Ezra, Jeremiah, Ezekiel, Isaiah and Galatians though Revelation. These books express the Sovereignty of God over all the earth, governments and individuals. Until we really get a picture of the Sovereignty of God we don't understand just how deep-seated our rebellion is. It is not me, myself and I that can do battle with the enemy; it is only through total surrender to the Almighty God of the universe that I can walk, run or soar. [4] His grace is sufficient for me for His strength is made perfect in my weakness![5] The onslaught of the enemy has lasted approximately three and a half years and yes at times I wondered if I could really be saved. But God is faithful, and that good work He began in me He will complete. [6] You see, the enemy of my soul didn't want chapter fifteen or the rest of this book to be written, much less having it published. Has the enemy left? No, and he will not. Do thoughts of condemnation still come? Yes! Is the Word more powerful than a two edged sword?[7] YES! It's the only way to combat the devil; quoting Scripture just as Jesus did when He fought the devil.[8] We must follow Jesus example in life or we become pawns in the hands of Satan. Jesus said follow Me,[9] lay your life down for My sake. [10] I heard someone say recently if you want to do what Jesus did-Do What Jesus Did. For that reason and that reason alone can I take this life one day at a time trusting that Jesus is LORD. One day He will take me from this life into His loving arms and I will spend eternity with Him. How do I know that? God is not a man that He should lie. [11]

Earlier I stated that faith is the key that unlocks the door and faith is the key that opens the door. *"Without faith it is IMPOSSIBLE to please Him (God); for he that cometh to God* MUST BELIEVE *that He is, and that He is a rewarder of them that* DILIGENTLY *seek Him."* [12] You see the enemy's number one tactic is: "Get them to doubt God and God's Word." [13] If you will doubt God's Word you naturally doubt Him; therefore, the Psalmist says this: *"I will worship toward thy holy temple, and praise thy name for thy loving kindness and for thy truth: for thou hast magnified thy word above all thy name."* [14]

SO, WHY IS SATAN STILL AROUND?

As you have seen by now, we have been given much power. Since God has given us this power there must be a reason for it. Remember what God had commanded Adam and Eve in the Garden of Eden: have dominion over the earth and subdue it. [15] He told Cain to subdue the sin that was crouching at the door to master him. I have shown through the Scripture that Jesus Christ not only came to 'take away sin' [16] but to 'fulfill all righteousness.' [17] Then He left and went back to heaven 'reigning till His enemies are under His feet. [18] Who do you suppose is going to put His enemies under His feet? And why do you think Christians are still being tempted by Satan not to believe God's Word? Through the writing of this book and the revelations of Scripture I have come to believe that Jesus Christ is going to put all enemies under His feet through the church-His body-as ambassadors. [19] Remember that He is the head and we are His body. Because we through surrender to the Holy Spirit are to subdue the enemy in this life, in us, in our relations, community and world! How are we to do this? Only through TOTAL submission to God through Prayer and Obedience!

Even as I write this book, God is revealing this to me daily in greater and greater ways. I'm learning to get up and take authority over my situations. God has allowed me to meet a man who began twenty-five to thirty years ago to take the Word of the Bible literally; he is walking in power; subduing the enemy his life and in the lives of others, bringing about deliverance, and healing through the Word. I had already written all but these last few chapters of this book when I met him and God has confirmed to me that I was on the right track with this writing. As a matter of fact I am only beginning to learn how to walk in this realm. I am learning to submit to every God given authority.[20] So how do we implement this power? We do this through prayer, trust, and continual confession of His Word.

CHAPTER SIXTEEN

[1] Genesis 3:1
[2] Hebrews 6:11-12
[3] 1 Peter 1:6-7
[4] Isaiah 40:31
[5] 2 Corinthians 12:9
[6] Philippians 1:6
[7] Hebrew 4:12
[8] Matthew 4:4-11
[9] Matthew 8:22; 9:9; Mark 8:34;
[10] John 12:24-26
[11] Numbers 23:19
[12] Hebrews 11:6
[13] Genesis 3:1 & 2 Corinthians 11:3
[14] Psalm 138:2
[15] Genesis 1:28
[16] John 1:29
[17] Matthew 3:15
[18] 1 Corinthians 15:24-25
[19] 2 Corinthians 5:20-21
[20] James 4:7, Ephesians 5:22, Romans 13:1, Titus 3:1, and 1Peter 2:13

Chapter Seventeen

Prayer

As I stated in the last chapter submission through prayer and obedience is how we are to subdue the enemy. We will discuss prayer and what it is. Even the disciples questioned Jesus on how to pray, they recognized that somehow they were inadequate when it came to prayer. His response is what is commonly referred to as the Lord's Prayer. [1] In studying it here are some thoughts gleaned from the Scripture references in the concordance of my Bible:

First Jesus said, don't be like hypocrites, then listed several things a hypocrite would do, such as pray only in public to be seen of men, use repetitious prayers and lots of vain words, not showing any type of relationship to God. They may have only used written prayers that were written by others and may sound pious or lofty.

Then notice He said pray like this:

- *Our Father:* 1st Principle- First and foremost we pray to the Father in Jesus' name, we do not pray to anyone else, i.e., Mary or a 'Saint,' Jesus said you won't need to ask me anything, pray to the Father. [2] Second, know God as your Father-recognize it's a relationship, someone you are intimate with. Jesus said in John 16:27 that the Father loves us because we have loved Him (Jesus), and believed He came from the Father. Also note it is OUR, the corporate body-you're not in it by yourself, we are members in particular.
- *Hallowed be Thy name:* 2nd Principle- Always keep sacred; honor and reverence His "name"- YHWY or Yahweh. In Leviticus 10:3 God told Moses to tell Aaron those who come near to Him '*must*' regard

Prayer

Him as holy and He must be glorified before all people. So use His name only for worship, evangelism, or prayer.
- *Thy kingdom come:* 3rd Principle- Jesus said in Romans 14:17 that the kingdom of God is righteousness, peace and joy. Jesus took our sin and gave us His righteousness. [3] Then in Hebrews it is stated that we are receiving a kingdom. [4] 2 Peter tells us to add certain things to our faith then states we need to make our call and election sure so that we will be able to enter into the everlasting kingdom.[5] Jesus said in Matthew 6:13 *"It has been given to you to know the mysteries of the kingdom of heaven."* The kingdom will come in the earth in and through us as we yield to the Holy Spirit, but He wants us to desire it and ask for it to come.
- *Thy will be done on earth as it is in heaven:* 4th Principle-Ask God to make His will your will; submit to God in everything, asking for His will in every area of your life. We are to be just as obedient as the angels in heaven are. They fulfill God's commands immediately. God says that obedience is better than sacrifice and rebellion is as the sin of witchcraft. [6] It would serve us well to walk in obedience to the Word of God, thus bringing His kingdom in the earth.
- *Give us this day our daily bread:* 5th Principle-Understand that God is our supplier, He may use different sources of supply, but He is the supplier. 2 Peter 1:3-4 says His divine power has supplied everything we need for life and godliness. We only look to Him trusting His for His provision on a daily basis, keep the relationship current: daily. This is not only food but all provision, money, health, and the bread of His Word, etc.
- *And forgive us our debts, as we forgive our debtors:* 6th Principle- God desires mercy and not sacrifice; [7] we are to bear with others and forgive others just like Christ has forgiven us. [8] In Matthew 18 there is a story about a man who was forgiven much, but did not forgive a small debt owed to him. When his master found out he took all he had and delivered him, his wife and children to the torturers' until all could be paid. Jesus said His Father in heaven would do the same thing to those who refuse to forgive others.
- *And do not lead us into temptation, but deliver us from evil:* 7th Principle-Satan is after you. If you belong to Christ, he doesn't want you to be victorious. We need to be vigilant because he's out to devour us. [9] The Hebrew translation of this portion of Scriptures says this. 'Lead us not into hard testing'- God does test us in our walk, see Job 1, and remember the testing I went through for over three years. Jesus

Christianity

is saying 'let it not be hard.' He will never put on us more than we can bear (sometimes, we just don't know how much we can bear.) Then it says to deliver us from the evil one. [10]

- *For Thine is the Kingdom, and the power, and the glory forever:* 8th Principle- It's all about God. It's not about me and mine.[11]

I have come to understand prayer is not only petition, but declaration as well. It is not just thinking or silently mouthing the words. Prayer, is total submission in communion with God, giving God our undivided attention. Prayer is not only literally talking, speaking words out loud, just as if you could literally see God the Father and/or Jesus and/or the Holy Spirit sitting in our presence, but it is listening for a response. In any conversation you talk out loud and you listen; you don't just sit and think what you are going to say-you speak it out. Proverbs tells us there is death and life in the power of the tongue or spoken word.[12] In the book of James, we are told the tongue sets on fire the course of nature. [13] Those two scriptures are not referring to what is going on in your mind. It is referring to actual speaking things aloud. When Jesus prayed we know He spoke aloud, He went 'off' early in the morning to pray.[14] Hebrews 4:12 says; *"The Word of God is living and active and powerful...."* How is it so powerful just lying on a table or on a book shelf? What has your Bible done for you lately as it lies on your table? In Isaiah, the prophet says, the Lord says,*"I have sworn by Myself;* <u>The word has gone out of My mouth</u> *in righteousness, and will not return, That unto Me every knee shall bow, every tongue will swear.*[15] And again He says, *"For as the rain and snow come down from heaven, and do not return there without watering the earth and make it bear and sprout, and furnish seed to the sower and bread to the eater; so will My <u>word be which goes forth from My mouth</u>; it will not return to Me empty, without accomplishing what I desire, and without succeeding in the matter for which I sent it."* [16] As ambassadors of Jesus Christ, we take His Word and pray, speak it back to Him in faith (trusting) that it will accomplish what He spoke it to be. In doing this we accomplish three things; first as we speak His Word aloud bringing it to His remembrance, we are hiding it in our heart. [17] At the same time it is building our faith [18] causing us to trust in what He has said He will do. Lastly it is moving heaven and earth to accomplish His purpose, [19] because we are His ambassadors [20] and the purpose of an ambassador is to accomplish the purpose of the one whom he is under authority in his stead.

Prayer

For example: If I am praying for someone's salvation I may pray:

Father your Word says in John 3:16 that *"You are not willing that any should perish (be lost) but have everlasting life"* so I bring _____ before You and ask that You send the Holy Spirit [21] to 'remove the blinders the god of this age has put over _____ eyes so they cannot see the light of the gospel of the glory of Christ.'[22] Father may the Holy Spirit convict _____ of sin and 'bring them to repentance that _____ may come to their senses, come to know the truth and escape out of the snare of the devil where ___ has been taken captive by him to do his will' and that ___ be saved. [23] I am trusting [24] Your Word to accomplish [25] _____ salvation and through Your Spirit _____ is 'delivered from the kingdom of darkness and translated into the Kingdom of Your dear Son,'[26] In Jesus name.

In praying like this we are (as His body, His mouth) taking His Word, speaking it in faith (trust) that it be brought it to pass. In speaking His Word, His will is accomplished. Remember that faith (trust) is the confident persuasion that the ultimate (last in a progression) reality which causes the outward manifestation and change, it WILL TAKE PLACE. Hence we must never confess anything contrary to that prayer. Always speak what God's Word says. Confession is a big part of the battle. It is the engaging in battle through the Word offensively-Sword of the Spirit. This is warfare. The enemy will do everything he can to stop this so we must be persistent. This is where many of us fail in our walk. We allow the enemy to get us to take our eyes off the Word and the promises and begin to confess what we see with our physical eyes and that negates the Word we have prayed. When the doubt comes in it brings in double-mindedness. [27] It is in the constant confession of the Word (faith in action) prayed over someone that 'the prayer of a righteous man will avail much.' [28] For reasons known only to God their salvation may take years, but His Word is truth and will not return to Him void. Our job is to believe, i.e., trust, it's the Spirit's job to do the work in them. Let me also add, the importance of praise. *"God inhabits the praise of His people."*[29] When, and how much, we praise God for bringing about the petition we have brought before Him will let Him know whether or not we truly believe He is working to bring about the answer.

CHAPTER SEVENTEEN

[1] Matthew 6:5-15
[2] John 16:23-26[2]
[3] 2 Corinthians 5:21
[4] Hebrews 12:28
[5] 2 Peter 2:11 see previous verses also
[6] 1 Samuel 15:22-23
[7] Matthew 9:13
[8] Colossians 3:13
[9] 1 Peter 5:8
[10] 2 Peter 2:9
[11] 1 Corinthians 15:28 and Philippians 3:21
[12] Proverbs 18:21
[13] James 3:6
[14] Hebrews 5:7
[15] Isaiah 45:23
[16] Isaiah 55:10-11[4]
[17] Psalm 119:11
[18] Jude 20
[19] Isaiah 55:10-11
[20] 2 Corinthians 5:20
[21] John 16:8
[22] 2 Corinthians 4:4
[23] 2 Timothy 2:25
[24] James 1:6
[25] Isaiah 5:11
[26] Colossians 1:13
[27] James 1:6-7
[28] James 5:16
[29] Psalm 22:3

Chapter Eighteen

The Lord's Supper or The Eucharist

"He (Jesus) said to them, "With fervent desire I have desired to eat this Passover with you before I suffer; for I say to you, I will no longer eat of it until all is fulfilled in the kingdom of God." Then He took the cup, and gave thanks, and said, "Take this and divide it among yourselves; for I say to you, I will not drink of the fruit of the vine until the kingdom of God comes." And He took bread, gave thanks and broke it, and gave it to them, saying, "This is My body which is given for you; do this in remembrance of Me." Likewise He also took the cup after supper, saying, This cup is the new covenant in My blood, which is shed for you."[1]

The LORD's Supper is a solemn assembly; it is not to be taken lightly because it represents Jesus' suffering for our sin. It was on this night of the Hebrew Passover that Jesus and the disciples, commemorated the Exodus from Egypt, which was pointing forward to the death and resurrection of Jesus that would deliver us from sin once for all. It was this Passover, the Eucharist or LORD's Supper that was instituted for Christians. For the Hebrews it was a looking back to the Exodus, for Christians it is looking back to Jesus death and resurrection. It is in taking the bread and juice that we proclaim His suffering for our personal sin. Therefore, the elements should only be taken by those who have made Jesus Christ Lord, i.e., Master. Paul warns us not to take the Eucharist lightly. Many churches practice 'open' communion where anyone including children are allowed to take the elements. While I don't suggest 'closed' communion, there should be a solemn warning concerning partaking in an unworthy manner as well as instruction as to who should take communion. (This is why many churches practice closed communion, which is communion taken only by 'members' of that particular body. This in their eyes will prohibit unworthy consumption.) Many people feel like if they have been baptized or are a member of a/the 'church' they are justified in taking part in the service without regard to any sin in their lives. So let's look at how the Amplified Bible instructs the partaking of this ordinance: *"For every time you eat this bread and drink this cup, you are representing and signifying and proclaiming the fact of the Lord's death until He comes [again]. So then whoever eats the bread or drinks the cup of the Lord in a way that is unworthy [of Him] will be guilty of [profaning and sinning against] the body and blood of the Lord. Let a man [thoroughly] examine himself, and [only when he has done so] should he eat of the bread and drink of the cup*. For anyone who eats and **drinks without discriminating and recognizing with due appreciation** *that [it is Christ's] body*, **eats and drinks a sentence (a verdict of judgment) upon himself**. *That [careless and unworthy participation] is the reason many of you are weak and sickly, and quite enough of you have fallen into the sleep of death*. **For if we searchingly examined ourselves** *[detecting our shortcomings and recognizing our own condition]*, **we should not be judged and penalty decreed** *[by the divine judgment]. But when we [fall short and] are judge by the Lord, we are disciplined and chastened*, **so that we may not [finally] be condemned [to eternal punishment along] with the world.** [2] There are a couple of things I want to draw your attention to in this Scripture. First, regarding children: how can a child thoroughly examine himself, not knowing Scripture (I speak of many who are too young to even understand sin)? Secondly, how often is there a 'waiting', a thorough personal examination before taking the elements? I have witnessed talking, looking around and a lack of sacredness while the Scripture is read and the elements passed, as if waiting in line at the grocer until everyone gets the elements; no quiet, reverent, examination, no searching for a sin much less repenting before partaking. We wonder why many are sick and cannot receive healing, why many are weak and unable to battle with the enemy in the body of Christ and why some die prematurely. Could this possibly have something to do with it? Are we profaning and sinning against the body of Christ?

I believe we are not only to thoroughly examine our own hearts but wait that others may examine themselves so that if forgiveness is needed

the Lord's Supper Or The Eucharist

of one from whom an offense has been received or possibly given and only when all is reconciled should the elements be taken.

I would also add here that in years past many churches had foot washing services (men and women separate) generally after the partaking of The LORD's supper because it was part of the Last Supper. Foot washing represents our willingness to serve our brothers and sisters in humbleness before Christ, thus not allowing pride or 'lording it over' attitudes to prevail in our congregations. Jesus told Peter if he did not let Him wash his feet, he had no part in Him. I personally believe this would bring about a greater fellowship and stronger bond with those with whom we fellowship. I have participated in many of these services and I know it is not only humbling to wash another's feet but also allowing others to wash my feet. As a matter of fact it is in the receiving that is most humbling.

CHAPTER EIGHTTEEN

|1| Luke 22:15-20[8]
|2| 1 Corinthians 11:26-32[1]

QUESTIONS TO PONDER BY CHAPTER

CHAPTER ONE
1. Why is Christianity so important? Why become a Christian?

2. What is God's purpose for the restoration of man?

3. What did Jesus' death make possible?

CHAPTER TWO
1. What two words describe the Bible?

2. Do you have to believe the Bible is true to be a Christian? Why?

CHAPTER THREE
1. Who is God? Can we know everything about Him?

2. What are some names of God? What is God's name in Hebrew? How did we get these names?

3. What is Jesus relationship with God? What is His position in the Godhead? What is Jesus name in Hebrew? What does it mean?

4. Who is the Holy Spirit? What is the function of the Holy Spirit?

5. What is the Trinity? Is it mentioned in the Bible?

CHAPTER FOUR
1. What was God's pattern for making man? Is there a difference between 'image' and 'likeness'?

2. What is your soul? How did Adam receive his soul?

3. How was the creation of Eve different from Adam?

4. What does 'help-meet' mean?

5. What role did God give Adam and Eve in the beginning?

6. What was His first command? What does the word 'let' have to do with it?

7. Did God establish marriage with Adam and Eve?

CHAPTER FIVE
1. Who is Satan? Where did he come from? Does he have a kingdom?

2. What are some of the names of Satan? What is his character?

3. Does he have a following? Where did they come from?

Questions To Ponder By Chapter

4. Is Satan subject to anyone? Whom? Can he do anything he wants to man? What is his end?

CHAPTER SIX

1. What command did God give Adam when He placed him in the Garden?

2. What did the serpent tell Eve to get her to eat of the fruit? Where was Adam?

3. Did Adam and Eve 'reason' before the Serpent tempted them in the garden?

4. What did God do to the serpent? What was the curse on the serpent? How would his relationship with Eve affect all humanity?

5. How did God curse Eve? What change in her role with Adam took place? How would that affect their relationship?

6. How did Adams role change? How did the word 'let' come into play in this circumstance?

7. What was God's statement concerning why He must send Adam and Eve out of the Garden? Can you think of what might have happened if they had eaten of the fruit of the Tree of Life now?

CHAPTER SEVEN

1. What three things describe the essence of sin? What New Testament Scripture list them?

2. What caused Satan's fall?
3. What did Satan tell Eve she could be like if she ate the fruit?

Christianity

4. *What words did Scripture use when pronouncing the curse on Eve as it did when God was talking to Cain about sin ruling over him?*

5. *How long did it take for man to become exceedingly sinful to the point of grieving God? Just how sinful were they-what does Genesis 6:5 say about man?*

6. *What words used in Genesis 6 expressed God's repentance?*

CHAPTER EIGHT

1. *What is Salvation? Is there a difference between the meaning in the Old and New Testaments? If so what?*

2. *In order for one to be saved he must be_____? How does one get to that place?*

3. *What is the cost of Salvation? Is it free?*

4. *What does the phrase 'right to become' mean?*

5. *According to Webster's Dictionary and Strong's Concordance what does the word 'become' mean?*

6. *In Salvation what happens to 'the old nature'? What did I relate this to? Who did Paul say would deliver him from 'this body of death'?*

7. *What is adoption according to Baker's Evangelical Dictionary of Biblical Theology?*

8. How does Roman adoption and relate to our adoption into the family of God?

9. What does endure mean? How do you purify you soul?

10. What does estranged mean?

11. Give a one sentence definition of repentance.

CHAPTER NINE
1. Who is the only one that we can go to for our Salvation?

2. Give one word John the Baptist, Jesus and Peter used to call men to God?

3. What does it mean when John the Baptist said that Jesus came to "take away the sin of the world"?

4. What did God the Father do for our Salvation?

5. What did Jesus do for our Salvation?

6. What does the Holy Spirit do for our Salvation?

7. What four words describe our part?

CHAPTER TEN
1. What does it mean to be born again?

2. What is one thing we must do before we can be born again?

3. What happened to the sin nature when we identified with the death of Jesus?

4. What are the meanings of the four words for repentance in Scripture?

5. What is the 'fixed' basis of our death? What does that mean? What do we have to become 'convinced' of after repentance?

6. What does anything dead 'do'?

7. What did Paul in Romans tell us to consider when talking about our relationship to sin?

8. What does it mean that our hearts are circumcised?

9. If the Spirit of God is in you, what will you do that will bring about the process of sanctification?

CHAPTER ELEVEN

1. What is faith?

2. What does the word substance mean? How does that affect our lives?

3. Are we still 'sinners' saved by grace or does something happen to change who we are?

4. What does the word 'looking' mean? Does this have the same meaning as the word 'fix' in a previous chapter?

CHAPTER TWELVE

1. What is walking after the flesh? What does it mean to walk after the Spirit?

2. How does Paul explain in Roman seven that we are no longer under the law and the 'sin nature' after we receive Jesus as our Savior?

3. What happened to the angels who disobeyed God?

CHAPTER THIRTEEN

1. What is Jesus doing in heaven? Is He able to save us?

2. What 'fruit' should we be showing in our lives so that others will see Jesus?

3. What happens when a person draws back from God?"

4. Is the phrase 'once saved, always saved' Scriptural? Is it in the Bible? What does this doctrine imply?

5. Is there something about the word 'unto' that is important in understanding heart faith?

6. What does 'translate' mean? How does a 'pool' relate to Salvation and translate?

7. What did Jesus tell the man at the Pool of Bethesda and the woman caught in adultery?

8. What does God's 'justness' demand He do about continual sin in the life of a person?

9. Can a person 'fall from grace'? What is 'estranged' and what does it mean?

10. According to Hebrews six what are we doing to Christ if we continue to sin? Is it possible for a person to sin every day and be saved?

11. Who is responsible for our Salvation and understanding of the Bible?

12. What does the word 'let' have to do with sin in our lives?

13. What does 1 John 3:9 say?

CHAPTER FOURTEEN

1. What did Jesus say about being the Light of the World and us following Him?

2. How can quoting the Scripture over our lives give us victory?

3. What is the armor of God and how does Scripture help us implement it?

4. Why is Faith so important?

5. What do the words of our mouth do? How much power is in our tongue?

Chapter Fifteen

1. Why does the church look anemic today? Have the gifts of the Spirit ceased to be functional?

2. What did Jesus tell the disciples they needed to do to receive power? Do you think we need to do the same?

3. According to the list of Scriptures what has been provided for the believer?

4. Why do Christians need power?

Chapter Sixteen

1. What Scripture did God give me to let me know what had been happening in my life to get me off track? What was the test? Who test us? Who tempts us? What did the enemy want me to do?

2. What is more powerful than a two-edged sword?

3. How does that help us fight the enemy? Who gave us an example of using the Word as a sword?

4. What is necessary to please God?

5. Why does God want to give us power? What has God made us that we would need this power?

6. How are we to subdue the enemy?

CHAPTER SEVENTEEN
1. What is prayer? Why is it important?

2. What are the 8 principles of "The LORD's Prayer?

3. What are the two aspects of prayer?

4. As ambassadors for God how do we utilize prayer in accomplishing His will? When we use the Word whose mouth and body are we being?

5. Using the Word of God is like using a weapon, which one?

6. What does doubt produce in us? When we doubt what can we expect from God?

7. What does God inhabit?

CHAPTER EIGHTEEN
1. What is the 'Lord's Supper'? What has it to do with 'Passover'?

2. Who should participate in the Communion Service?

3. How are we to approach communion? What is the purpose of waiting?

4. What are some things Paul says happens as a result of not waiting and partaking the elements in an unworthy manner?

APPENDIX 1

The Italicized numbers after the Scripture on the Chapter reference pages are contributed to the following list:

1. Amplified Bible, Scriptures taken from the Holy Bible, Amplified Version. I used www.biblegateway.com/versions for Amplified translation of Scripture.
2. Scripture quotations marked NLT are taken from the Holy Bible, New Living Translation, copyright 1996, 2004, 2007. Used by permission of Tyndale House Publishers, Inc. Carol Stream, Illinois 60188. All rights reserved.
3. Adoption Summary taken from page 1552 of Scofield Study Bible, The Holy Bible, English Standard Version, copyright 2001 by Crossway Bibles, a division of Good News Publishers. All rights reserved.
4. Scripture taken from the New American Standard Bible, Copyright, 1960, 1962, 1968. 1071. 1972. 1973. 1975. 1977. 1995 by the Lockman Foundation
5. Scriptures taken from the Holy Bible, New International Version. Copyright 1973, 1978, 1984 International Bible Society. Used by permission of Zondervan Publishing House. All rights reserved.
6. Strong's Exhaustive Commentary, ISBN 0-917006-01-1, The Exhaustive Concordance of the Bible, by James Strong, S.T.D., LL.D., Hendrickson Publishers, Peabody, Massachusetts
7. Webster's Seventh New Colligate Dictionary based on Webster's Third New International Dictionary Copyright 1961, 1966, 1971.
8. Scripture taken from the New King James Version®. Copyright © 1982 by Thomas Nelson
9. James Lee Beall, Laying a Foundation, Pages 12-13
10. http://www.wordsmyth.net/draw

11. God's Plan For Man, Finis Jenning's Dake, Lesson two, Page 12, III What the Bible Is, third paragraph.
12. Baker's Evangelical Dictionary of Biblical Theology, Copyright © 1996 by Walter A. Elwell. Taken from http://www.biblestudytools.com/dictionaries/bakers-evangelical-dictionary/ **By permission of Oxford University Press, USA.** For electronic editions (URL www.oup.com)
13. Bible Dictionary, Webster's Encyclopedia of Dictionaries, Copyright 1958 by Literary Press. Ottenheimer Publisher Inc.

APPENDIX 2

Other Names of God

Jehovah Qadash – *Yeh-ho-vaw kaw-dash': to be made clean, ceremonially or morally consecrate, dedicate, defile, hallow (be, keep) holy, proclaim, purify, sanctify, wholly. The Lord who sanctifies you Exodus31:13, Lev. 20:8; 18:20; 22:32.*

JehovahTsidkenu – *Yeh-ho-vaw tsid-kay'-noo: The Lord our righteousness.* Psalms 4:1, Jeremiah 23:6.

Jehovah Nicciy-*Yeh-ho-vaw' nis-see': Jehovah my banner* Exodus 17:15.

Jehovah Rapha'-*Yeh-ho-vaw' raw-faw': Jahovah–to mend, repair, stitch, to make thoroughly whole.* Exodus 15:26.

Jehovah Shalom-*Yeh-ho-vaw' shaw-lome': Jehovah (is) peace* Isa. 9:6.
Jehovah Shammah –*Yeh-ho-vow' shawm'-maw: Jehovah (is) thither (here)* Gen 28:15, Ex 33:14; Daniel 20:1.

Adonai- adon- *aw-done': sovereign, i.e. controller (human or divine),*

El Roi – the God who sees – Gen 16:13.

APPENDIX 3

THE TRUE CHARACTER OF CHRISTIANS

A list of things in alphabetical order is stated about those whose hearts and minds are devoted the Christ Jesus:

Attentive to Christ's voice–John 10:3, 4

Blameless and harmless–Philippians 2:15

Bold–Proverbs 28:1; Ephesians 3:11-12

Contrite–Isaiah 57:15, 66:2

Devout–Acts 8:2; 22:12

Faithful–Revelation 17:14

Fearing God–Matthew 3:16, Acts 10:2

Following Christ–John 10:4, 27

Godly–Psalms 4:3; 2 Peter 2:9

Guileless–John 1:47

Holy–Deuteronomy 7:6; 14:2; Colossians 3:12

Humble–Psalms 34:2; 1 Peter 5:5

Hungering after righteousness–Matthew 5:6

Just–Genesis 6:9; Habakkuk 2:4; Luke 2:25

Led by the Spirit–Romans 8:14

Liberal with all he has–Isaiah 32:8, 2 Corinthians 9:13

Loving–Colossians 1:4; 1 Thessalonians 4:9

Lowly–Proverbs 16:19

Meek–Isaiah 29:19; Matthew 5:5
Merciful–Psalms 37:26; Matthew 5:7
New Creatures–2 Corinthians 5:17; Ephesians 2:10
Obedient–Romans 16:19; 1 Peter 1:14
Poor in spirit–Psalms 51:17; Matthew 5:3
Prudent–Proverbs 16:21
Pure in heart–Matthew 5:8; 1 John 3:3
Righteous–Isaiah 60:21; Luke 1:6
Sincere–2 Corinthians 1:12; 2:17
Steadfast–Acts 2:42; Colossians 2:5
Taught of God–Isaiah 54:13; 1 John 2:27
True–2 Corinthians 6:8
Undefiled–Psalms 119:1
Upright–1 Kings 3:6; Psalms 15:2
Watchful–Luke 12:37
Zealous of good works–Titus 2:14; 3:8

APPENDIX 4

THE BENEFITS OF THE NEW NATURE

Our Sins have been Taken Away — Forgiven–John 1:29 & Colossians 2:13
We are justified–Romans 3:24
Not Condemned–Romans 8:1
Set Free–Romans 8:2
We are a New Creation–2 Corinthians 5:17
Sanctified (set apart for a sacred purpose)–1 Corinthians 1:2
Made Alive By Resurrection–1 Corinthians 15:22
Have Received God's Righteousness–2 Corinthians 5:21
We Are One In Christ With All Believers–Galatians 3:28
Blessed with Every Spiritual Blessing–Ephesians 1:3
Holy, Blameless Covered with God's Love – Ephesians 1:4
Accepted in the Beloved–Ephesians 1:6
Gathered together with all things in Christ–Ephesians 1:10
Raised Up With Christ–Ephesians 2:6
God's Work of Art–Ephesians 2:10
Brought Near To God–Ephesians 2:13
Share In the Promise in Christ–Ephesians 3:6
We have the Freedom & Confidence to Come to God–Ephesians 3:12
Members of Christ's Body — The Church–Ephesians 5:30, 27
We are made whole, full and complete In Christ–Colossians 2:10
We are delivered and set Free from Our Sinful Nature–Romans 6:18, 22 & 8:2
We have the promise of Eternal Glory–2 Timothy 2:10
We died with Him, we shall also live with Him and reign with Him–
2 Tim 2:11-12a

CPSIA information can be obtained
at www.ICGtesting.com
Printed in the USA
FFOW02n0157211215
19663FF